Multiplied

Multiplied

How digital transformation can deliver
more impact for the public sector

Ben Holliday

Foreword: Neal Gandhi

Executive Editor: Sarah Finch

Managing Editor: Rob Prevett

ISBN: Paperback: 978-1-80227-411-0
eBook: 978-1-80227-410-3

This book is dedicated to everyone working across our public sector, acknowledging the incredible effort and responses that we have seen during the Covid-19 pandemic.

All profits will be donated to the Association of NHS Charities.

nhscharitiestogether.co.uk

Acknowledgements

"Multiplied" has been deliberately written in a non-singular voice ("we" not "I"). This is because this book has only been made possible because of the knowledge, experience and hard work of my colleagues at TPXimpact. Specifically, the content and themes covered have been informed by work, direct contributions, and feedback from Anna Inman, Bryony Wilde, Claire Hazelgrove, David Ayre, David Thompson, Gavin Bell, Imeh Akpan, James Herbert, Jen Byrne, Jonathan Flowers, Loren Hansi Gordon, Martin Wright, Matt Jukes, Matt Skinner, Natalie Taylor, Rob Bates, Sarah Finch, Sat Ubhi, Simon Wakeman, Stef Webb, Stuart Arthur and Zung Nguyen Vu.

To Neal Gandhi, thank you for the support you've shown throughout the process of creating this book. Not only in creating the time and space to write it, but for leading a company that gives us a platform for doing the types of work we have been able to share.

Conor Moody and Liberty-Belle Howard, thank you for your efforts in reading, proofing and sense checking final edits of the book. And finally I'd like to thank Sarah Finch and Rob Prevett for the many hours spent working tirelessly reviewing chapters, questioning and challenging the thinking and ideas to get us to a finished manuscript. A true team effort . . .

I hope this starts a bigger conversation!

Ben Holliday, January 2022

Contents

Foreword by Neal Gandhi

In 2020, everything we took for granted was upended. The way society and communities worked, learnt and interacted was transformed overnight. How people shopped, socialised and entertained changed radically. For many, the nature of work changed in a few short hours. Office workers were sent home and asked to carry on as normally as possible. Others were less fortunate, being furloughed, or losing their jobs entirely as whole sectors of the economy shut down.

A population scale experiment ensued that challenged the very nature of 20th century hierarchical work structures. In the absence of being able to look over people's shoulders, even the most traditional organisations had to trust people to get on with their work. On the whole, they responded spectacularly well. Work continued even though we struggled through social isolation, homeschooling and enduring uncertainty. In many cases, productivity improved, with people able to fit their work around their other commitments and time normally spent commuting used more effectively. For many, a new relationship between employers and employees began to form with trust at the heart. This mirrored the inspiring community response that we all saw and felt in our towns, villages and cities. That trust and mutuality were central to success.

At the sharp end of the Covid-19 pandemic, a stark contrast emerged between top down, centrally controlled, hierarchical approaches versus ground up, organic, lean approaches to solving the new and fast moving challenges that we faced.

Critical new services in policy areas like health and education were launched from scratch in a matter of days or weeks. Teams took a digital, agile approach to solve real world problems. Despite the urgency of the situation, Government Digital Service (GDS), and NHS Service Standards were followed with assessments completed in as little as 15 minutes. Multidisciplinary teams involving civil servants and external suppliers worked together with a sense of common purpose and urgency. Policymakers, digital and IT people worked together iteratively to come up with something that worked. Leadership trusted teams to deliver, which they did time and time again.

At TPXimpact we saw some spectacular successes including:

- NHS Home Testing, delivering home testing kits to NHS staff enabling those with symptoms but negative Covid-19 tests to return to work faster.
- Ventilator Dashboard for The Department for Business, Energy and Industrial Strategy (BEIS), bringing together manufacturers at the start of the pandemic to form ventilator manufacturing consortia.
- Food for Vulnerable programme for The Department for Environment, Food and Rural Affairs (Defra), connecting vulnerable and shielding citizens with supermarkets to access priority delivery slots.
- Camden Beacon, connecting shielding residents with local service providers to offer assistance where necessary.

While our media were obsessed with the large scale top down programmes that struggled, they failed to report on the hundreds, if not thousands of programmes of work that delivered meaningful outcomes in communities across our country.

Previous processes and ways of working that were embedded across the public sector, that had historically been used to mitigate against risk and to ensure collective ownership of decisions so future failure could not be attributed, were exposed as actually adding risk and increasing the chances of failure. Instead we saw the public sector at its best, working closely with private sector partners to deliver impactful services that truly delivered for citizens when they needed them most.

Many of our ways of working were conceived in a different era, at a time before the mass acceptance of cloud computing, open source, APIs and agile approaches. The pandemic showed us that not only were many historic approaches no longer fit for purpose, they were actually damaging, resulting in poor outcomes, and slower times to launch. Furthermore they were substantially more expensive compared to more progressive and modern approaches to designing and delivering public services.

As I've reflected on the wider lessons from our experience as a society since March 2020, I have become staunchly convinced that things don't have to revert back to the way they were before.

I believe it's now possible to deliver more in the public sector; more impact through better outcomes, delivered in less time and demonstrating far greater value to the taxpaying public.

And why do I believe this? Because I've seen it over and over again in our work. This is change supported by technology, designed and working with communities, and fundamentally reshaping our public institutions.

This book explains how the public sector can learn the lessons from the pandemic and institutionalise the power of Multiplied Thinking to deliver time and again. In doing so, we can deliver public services that will underpin a rewiring of our nation and a post pandemic reinvention for future generations.

Neal Gandhi, CEO TPXimpact, January 2022

Introduction

This book is for anyone that creates, delivers or supports public policy and services. It's about what the public sector, and everyone working with the public sector, does next, the future of digital transformation, and what we can learn from the biggest crisis in our lifetimes to date – the Covid-19 pandemic.

Most of the contributors to the chapters that follow have worked in the civil service, or have led teams in government and across the UK health service. In writing this book the intention is to start new conversations, sharing ideas and insights from the work we have been part of, both before, and during the pandemic. As we have seen more clearly than ever, we all have a role to play in shaping how things change, and the opportunity to do things better.

The central idea of Multiplied is that far greater impact in people's lives is possible through public services. The challenge for us all is this: everything we have done so far, everything that can be learned from the pandemic response, and the years of digital transformation that preceded it, now gives us an opportunity to reevaluate our work and to question how we need to organise and work together in the future.

Multipliers

The themes we are about to explore build on existing ways of working, recognising that expectations have been reset over the course of how services have been delivered, and how organisations have responded since March 2020.

What is important here is understanding what has the potential to increase the reach and impact of the public sector's work. We call these multipliers – the things that make us more than the sum of our individual and collective parts.

To explore this further, we will cover the following themes in the next ten chapters. Each has the potential to be a multiplier when used or combined in new and creative ways.

- **People**: The importance of starting with user needs, and focusing on the outcomes services create, along with the impact the public sector has in all of our lives.
- **Teams**: How the people working inside our organisations can deliver far greater impact when aligned around shared goals and values, organising in new ways, and enabled by modern technology.
- **Participation:** Putting citizens' lived experience and voices at the heart of change to deliver far greater impact for people and the places they live. This is the potential for solutions to be more flexible and tailored around individual circumstances.
- **Inclusion:** Creating solutions that reach further, and that are more adaptable to everyone, making them accessible in the largest possible range of situations.
- **Research:** Working with insights from real life situations, understanding needs and context to deliver services that work best for people. Including working with people and communities who might otherwise find themselves excluded or adversely affected by the impact of policy and services.
- **Design**: Taking a first principles approach to understand and

reconfigure how public services work. Applying creative, visual approaches to support change, and learning by doing.

- **Technology**: Working with the right foundation of modern technologies, enabling organisations to effectively respond to change. Experimenting with new ways to build, configure and create value with technology.
- **Data**: Creating increasingly personalised services and experiences, built around personal data and insight, providing more relevant and meaningful interactions with the public sector.
- **Delivery**: Adapting and building on agile ways of working to deliver change faster, demonstrating and creating value incrementally.
- **Knowledge:** Working together, and in the open, through the sharing of insights and ideas, and with collaboration across services and new technology platforms.

All of these things are key to how digital transformation can deliver more impact for the public sector, and putting this into practice will depend upon our ability to think and act differently. But most of all, we need to put people at the centre of everything we do. The impact of public services is found in the experience of the individuals who use them every day. It is in the places in which we live and work, and in the way we interact with our communities as we go through our lives.

As we move into a new era of digital transformation, now is the time to be bold and to reset our expectations for what is possible.

Part 1

Impact

1 Impact multiplied

"Claiming that something is impossible is nothing more than a temporary working hypothesis. Two plus two can equal five if something changes."

– Arne Naess[1]

Every decision, and every action, taken in the public sector can make a positive difference to people's lives and to society. Impact is experienced and felt through policy, in the things services help us to do, how they support us individually, and how they shape the places we live.

To say that something impacts a person, situation or process simply means that something changes it in some way. In the context of the public sector, impact is a crucial concept as it's a measure of our ability to affect, shape or influence what happens.

We believe that this is an incredibly important way of analysing activity in the public sector, as it connects change to the people and places who live through it. Through focusing on impact, we can see how the forces of change – and the public sector's response to that change – affect people's lives.

As public servants, it could be that our goal is to lower carbon emissions, reduce child poverty, or shorten service waiting times. All of these aims can be approached with individuals in mind. What will be people's experience of these changes? How will they feel? What are the repercussions for other areas of their lives?

Living through change, and working with change

The public sector has a vital role in shaping and supporting what happens as everyone in society lives through change. Recent history provides a very clear example of this point. The lockdowns and lives lost since March 2020 have been a wake up call to how suddenly global changes can affect individual lives.

But having to adapt to change happening around us isn't new. Change, and often significant change, is actually a constant. Even outside of, and before, the Covid-19 pandemic, we have all been living through an era of accelerating environmental, cultural and technological change. We have experienced significant digital disruption as technology has reshaped our 21st century lives, with new types of services upending entire industries.

The technological advances that have fuelled this Fourth Industrial Revolution have enabled vast progress, but it's also worth noting that they don't affect people equally. The rapid pace of change has been uncomfortable for those without the skills, jobs or opportunities to operate in this new reality. We will see a similar pattern of inequality as we address other major global events – including the climate emergency – which we were only beginning to face up to as Covid-19 hit. It's an unfortunate fact that across the world, individuals and communities aren't all able to adapt to or deal with change in the same way.

This is the opportunity. If you're reading this book, the chances are that you have a role, or an interest in shaping the stories people will be able to tell about how public policy and services have impacted their lives. As we hope it becomes increasingly clear, inside or outside of a global emergency like Covid-19, our choices and the roles we play

– individually and collectively – have the potential to influence what happens next.

The challenge is how we organise and approach this work in a way that will deliver the best possible outcomes for individuals and their communities. How we ensure solutions are tailored to people and places with different types of needs, facing different types of situations, as we all experience continued global and societal change together. This is important for all of us, but particularly for those who rely on public services because they simply don't have anywhere else to turn.

The idea of impact multiplied

The central idea set out in this book is that it's possible to multiply the impact of work in the public sector. That by embracing modern ways of working, and through the use of design, technology and data, the impact and scale of our work can go far beyond what was previously thought to be achievable.

The quote at the beginning of this chapter states that anything is possible if something changes.

So what can change? Global events happening around us, such as the Covid-19 pandemic, lead us to respond in new and different ways. And just as importantly, there is our ability to make new things happen within existing systems and situations. This is our willingness to reset the rules, challenge constraints, and reframe problems.

Digital transformation working harder and reaching further

When it comes to digital transformation, things like the greater connectivity of the internet, cloud computing, and automation can all act as multipliers. These are all specific tools or approaches that enable us to do more. This means that small teams working in the right ways can deliver greater impact than hundreds of individuals following traditional approaches. With the right mindset and expertise, our digital transformation efforts become much more powerful. We will come back to how technology, as well as new ways of working, including research and service design, can help us to meet challenges head on.

More impact enabled by technology is also about reach. Digital transformation must ensure that no one, or no group of people is cut off from support; and that future services are adaptable to changing and emerging needs. No one should be left behind.

This is about making services increasingly accessible, inclusive, and adaptable to individual circumstances and situations, many of which we're not yet able to foresee because of the unpredictable nature of change.

As we think about future challenges, Covid-19 has shown how quickly public policy and services can change, forming rapid responses to fast moving events. In this first chapter we will now take a closer look at the foundations for delivering more impact – starting with how we can build on more than a decade of digital transformation in the public sector.

Legacy digital transformation

The digital transformation of public services is not a new idea. When we talk about digital transformation, we mean how organisations have adopted digital technologies and ways of working to respond to changing expectations for how people interact with public services.[2]

In the UK, we're fortunate to have such a significant digital legacy to build on from more than a decade of work. To recap and remind ourselves briefly of where we are:

The Government Digital Service

The Government Digital Service (GDS) was founded as the result of Martha Lane Fox's report into digital government in 2010.[3] While GDS wasn't the beginning of digital transformation in government, it has been a key catalyst for change over the past decade. GOV.UK was created as a single site bringing content and services from across UK government into one place for the first time. GDS had a clear digital by default strategy supported by a new Service Standard and design principles, maintained through spend control over technology projects, and with the introduction of service assessments as part of agile delivery.

GDS went on to deliver a programme of 25 exemplar projects in partnership with government departments (focusing on some of the highest volume transactional services on GOV.UK). These changed how people were able to access important services such as Lasting Power of Attorney, and Carer's Allowance, making services simpler, clearer and faster to use. Following this work – with successes, as well as a number of lessons learned – GDS's strategy increasingly switched focus from GOV.UK to the development of Government as a Platform (GaaP). Products developed have so far have included GOV.UK Verify, Pay, and Notify (again, with successes, and lessons learned). We have also seen the continued development and investment in cross government resources like the GOV.UK Design System.

Health

While GDS has made significant progress in UK government, the digital transformation of the health service has also taken significant steps. Delivered before GDS was founded, NHS.UK was originally launched in 2007 as NHS Choices. This brought together information about services, conditions, treatments, and medicines, as well as health improvement advice for the first time online, all under the trusted NHS brand. NHS

Digital is now responsible for providing digital services for the NHS and social care. As well as running NHS.UK since 2016, they have built and launched a number of products including NHS 111 online.

In 2019, along with the publication of the NHS Long Term Plan[4], NHSX was founded as a joint unit of NHS England and the Department of Health and Social Care. Working alongside NHS Digital, and with other organisations across the health system, the NHSX remit is to support local NHS Trusts and care organisations as they digitise services, and to transform patient outcomes and experiences through technology at home, in the community and in hospitals.

At the time this book was being completed it was announced that NHS Digital and NHSX are set to be merged into NHS England as part of a combined Transformation Directorate.[5]

Local authorities

Adopting GDS style digital delivery, there have been significant transformation programmes in local authorities across the country. Facing increased demand for services as well as pressures to find cost savings, parts of local government have responded time and again to the challenges of running front line services. Over the last decade, local authorities have worked hard to ensure that front line services including housing, adult social care, and children's services have continued to support the most vulnerable people in our society.

Much of this progress has been made by a community of people coming together as LocalGov Digital with best practice being shared organically through events like LocalGovCamp (first held in 2009 and pre GDS).[6] We have also seen local authorities and central government coming together through the Local Digital Declaration to reshape how technology is commissioned and built, challenging previous supplier monopolies and dependencies on enterprise software and legacy IT solutions.

Progress supported by digital delivery and new skills

To summarise the progress that has been made, organisations from across the public sector and their partners have demonstrated that they can use technology in new ways to improve access to services, streamline costs, and focus time and resources on the creation of new digital channels, often with an emphasis on self service and more automated, improved tools, systems and processes for staff. Increasingly this type of change, and the types of design, development and solutions that it requires, is something that can be delivered faster using agile approaches. And the tools, technologies and methods connected with digital transformation have become more accessible to more organisations than ever before.

To support this work, there has been a major shift with organisations increasingly adopting agile delivery, design, and product focused ways of working. This includes sector wide progress around increasing investment for in house digital and specialist capabilities, with representation for practice areas and skill sets such as engineering, data science, service design and user research. Most of these types of roles were previously only found outside the public sector, or were costly third party supplier dependencies.

To support the move to new specialist job roles and professions, GDS also led the work to create the Digital, Data, and Technology profession within the civil service from 2015 – helping all departments across government attract, develop and retain the people and skills they need for digital transformation.[7] A Digital Academy for upskilling and training civil servants, local government employees, devolved administrations and other public servants was first set up as part of the Department for Work and Pensions (DWP) in 2013. This later transitioned into the GDS Academy in 2017, and by 2019 over 10,000 students had been trained in new digital and delivery skills.[8]

A longer history of public sector reform

Digital transformation might have been the primary focus in many change programmes over the past decade, but the reform of our public institutions is nothing new. History shows us how different generations of politicians and leaders have responded to changing needs by investing in new initiatives. Just like today, many of these situations were the direct result of societal level disruption, with political leaders using crisis points as an opportunity to improve and reinvest in society. Perhaps the most well known of these was the formation of the National Health Service (NHS) in 1948, which was a much needed response following the Second World War.

For their part, public sector technology programmes and investments have been a response to the challenges of digital disruption, and the changing expectations for how modern organisations and services should work. Approaches such as design, product thinking, and agile delivery all represent different phases of this change, with each set of new ideas and methods building upon the last. As we will keep exploring, the challenge isn't to completely move away from these delivery methods. The opportunity is instead to refocus, applying new thinking. This is about building on what we have already learned, and – additionally – introducing new approaches, such as bringing increased community engagement into our programmes of work.

The digital transformation of the past ten to twenty years required a new type of mindset. It needed people that understood what it meant to live, work, and deliver services in the internet era. However, in the same way that we recognise any outdated technology as legacy, the digital transformation of the past can now be seen as legacy digital transformation. It represents a different era, designed for different types of context. We now need new approaches to build on this legacy in order to respond to current and future challenges. Mindsets must shift again to accommodate more radical change.

Taking a pandemic perspective

In the past decade, despite all the investments we have described in new digital skills, uses of technology and approaches such as agile delivery, changes to services have still been relatively slow and at times limited. The Covid-19 pandemic, which required fast and coordinated action to meet immediate needs, provides an interesting perspective on the history of digital transformation. Reflecting on our efforts during this period can help us to work out what we did successfully as well as what now needs to change.

The difference between digitising and digitalising

Too often, organisations and teams involved in digital transformation programmes have been constrained by what can best be described as digitisation – converting analogue solutions and processes into digital form. In this context, many services being transformed have, in fact, remained largely analogue but with an improved experience, user interface or digital front door added. In the public sector, digitisation has allowed us to do many of the same things, differently – moving analogue processes and transactional services online, but with very similar operating models, capabilities and processes inside our organisations.

While digitised services have made transacting online with government faster and easier, such solutions continue to feed into and rely upon legacy systems that require manual interventions and staff processing time. As such, they inevitably lead to data duplication and caseload backlogs that fall short of user expectations. It's not good enough, for example, for a service to take ten minutes to apply for online if it then takes weeks for the application to be processed by a member of staff. In an age of same day deliveries, when you can get approval for a credit card online in minutes, the frustration of public service users is understandable.

In contrast, digitalisation (a similar word, but with a very different meaning) is the focus on transforming business activities and services with technology. This is the opportunity to rethink how operations and capabilities can be completely reinvented, offering new possibilities and ways for organisations to create value.

During the pandemic we have seen more of a shift toward work we can start to describe as digitalisation. There has been increased demand for digital solutions, with the need to quickly create new types of services and share information online. This has included councils like Camden creating whole new services so that people could access different types of help when having to stay at home because of Covid-19. But just as importantly, we have also seen organisations accelerate their switch to better, more efficient, and dependable digital tools and systems, allowing a more flexible and adaptable workforce to respond to changing priorities on a daily basis.

Moving beyond digital

The goal of digital transformation should be to support how whole services deliver the best possible outcomes.

With technology, we can better meet user needs and expectations. At one level, this involves providing good user experiences, with seamless, pain free digital interactions. But technology is equally about automating systems, supporting staff processes, and transforming business activities. The full benefits of digital and technology are to be found when services are approached in this more holistic way.

Thanks to established design systems it has now become relatively straightforward to create digital interactions, including things like web based forms, notifications, and clearer online information and guidance. GOV.UK and sites like NHS.UK have led the way in this area, setting standards and providing resources for others to work with. But when we create these kinds of digital solutions, products, or tools for citizens or staff we are only ever solving part of a problem.

Services like housing, as well as employment, children's services, adults' services and health, all involve multiple and often recurring types of interactions. More importantly, they are structured around the relationships of the professionals who offer support, care and interventions. When we look closely, we find that all of these services are actually systems full of interdependencies. They are complex, involving the public, and, sometimes, the private sector as well.

Moving to the wholesale redesign of services means focusing on outcomes and how people move through these systems. To do this we have to understand a broader set of needs within communities. From improving employment and opportunities for young people within a specific local area, to helping more people find a long term place to live near their extended family, and making sure children are kept safe, we have to understand the complex relationships, interactions and circumstances individuals experience. In order to meet the needs people have in many of these scenarios, different partners will need to work together as part of larger systems to deliver the best possible outcomes within a range of sometimes extreme and fast changing situations.

During the pandemic we have seen the creation of entirely new services, including large scale initiatives to manage personal protective equipment (PPE), a national vaccination programme, and many examples of how local authorities have handled support in their communities. More often than not, such services were powered by volunteers, underpinned by technology and shared data wherever possible.

This work has been challenging, but is an example of the configuration of whole services, supported by technology both offline and online, and how organisations then work to meet needs in the most timely and efficient way possible.

Dealing with constraints and organisational silos

The impact of digital transformation has always been limited by different constraints.

In the public sector, the way digital is prioritised and delivered has often been the result of decisions taken elsewhere. Any positioning of policy or political intent as separate to the work of digital programmes is a significant challenge, as it limits the decisions teams are able to make. When digital is not closely linked to policy, or to the decision makers and strategists who actually determine how policy will be delivered, this limits the ability teams have to influence or change how services work, who can access them, and in what ways.

An inability to see policy or operational decisions that sit outside of digital transformation in the context of delivering a service has, so far at least, inevitably led to difficulties in scaling and sustaining digital change. The need has always been to design and scale operating models that are fully digitally enabled. The reality, though, is that it's been easier to navigate and prioritise easier problems to solve.

There is also a real human cost when there are gaps between policy, operations and delivery. When digital initiatives fail, or fail to go far enough, this is extremely tough on staff – the people very often holding our public institutions and front line services together. Understandably, we have met plenty of civil servants who will react with raised eyebrows and "not another change programme" in such situations. In the past, good intentions for digital transformation have left them with more work to do, feeling some short term impact if they're lucky, yet often with those costs offset somewhere else in a system that will have to be managed manually day by day.

The stories people share with us in our work are often about staff feeling that change is being done to them, rather than them being empowered to shape and contribute fully to what is happening. It isn't difficult to see the opportunity that is being missed, and that we should instead be building on the many years of experience, insights, and ultimately, public service of these individuals.

Throughout the pandemic we have seen the willingness, and necessity for people to work beyond existing constraints. Staff in organisations have stepped up to meet extraordinary challenges, maintaining and increasing levels of service in order to meet urgent needs, and all while also dealing with their own personal situations, challenges and anxieties. The truth is, however, that much of this workload is unsustainable, and the willingness of people to work more closely with colleagues and move beyond organisational boundaries has required additional effort. This needs to be recognised as we look to support people better in their jobs, sustainably, and with their future welfare in mind.

While the responses we have described so far might have been appropriate in an emergency, sometimes when you have to go faster the pace of change simply isn't sustainable. It's also not justifiable when we consider the pressure this puts on our teams and organisations. Sustaining longer term changes to how we work – in line with the new raised expectations of what is possible – will be hard.

The importance of rethinking what's possible with digital transformation has become increasingly clear because, throughout this crisis, we have seen how making changes to services and organisations helps us to reach people in communities. Digital tools and solutions have supported community action, enabling key things like food and medicine distribution, and ensuring that services provide support where it's most needed. We now need to consider how to reset in order to bring about this type of impact more permanently.

Resetting change

We have already introduced the idea that everything can change, and consequently, that anything is possible. But for many years this hasn't been the prevailing mindset in the public sector, as it has dealt with the politics of Brexit, austerity, and the complexity of delivering policy in a rapidly changing 21st century world.

On 3rd March, 2020, while working in local government, Simon Parker published a blog post that described the political landscape at the time, in particular, the challenges and ideological approaches being set out for civil service reform. Simon, now Director of Transformation and Policy Capability at the Department for Education (DfE), wrote, "Nothing can change. That phrase typifies so much of our politics at the moment. Social care is crumbling but nothing can change. The housing market is a mess but nothing can change. On climate and regional growth we are finally seeing the stirrings of some action, but I'm willing to bet if we push too hard we will find that not much can change there either."[9] While this quote taken in isolation might sound like defeatism, it can help us to understand how change does, or doesn't happen in relation to politics and our public policy and services.

This post was published before most of us had recognised what was about to happen over the coming months, right at the start of the Covid-19 pandemic. While the sentiment that nothing could change typified many political mindsets at the time, we have seen since that political change, and how it translates to policy and services, is possible with the right collective willpower.

To quote Simon again: "If we were really serious about building more houses, we would give councils and housing associations public money to get the job done. We would make land available for affordable housing. We would end street homelessness by having enough properties for a housing first approach. We literally did this after the Second World War." Looking back at Simon's post after several waves of Covid-19, we can reflect on how the pandemic has been a catalyst for change, just like the Second World War was in its time. Just as the post war government passed the New Towns Act to build houses, and established the National Health Service as a response to the effects of the war, we can now explore the possibilities as we continue to respond and recover from the biggest crisis in our own lifetimes. The question is also how this current crisis has enabled progress and change to happen at a faster pace and with more focus than ever before.

So if we look again at where our pandemic responses were successful, what changed that made fast and effective action possible?

1. Whole organisations prioritising digital transformation

The pandemic was the first time we have seen whole organisations fully prioritise digital transformation, rather than digital being delivered in a siloed way, detached from operational and policy teams.

The arrival of the pandemic broke down these barriers. It made people rethink fundamentals, and forced leaders to focus on what needed doing straight away – with the first priority to make more use of digital tools and channels to enable remote working. Where organisations needed to amend, or create new products or services as part of their pandemic response, traditional silos and organisational structures weren't allowed to get in the way. The push of the pandemic enabled a shift from very specific roles and responsibilities towards the collective ownership of problems that need solving immediately.

2. A new tolerance to managing and working with risk

There is an argument that both service providers, as well as service users, have been prepared to accept a greater level of risk during the pandemic. For citizens this is our willingness to allow access to personal data, required for solutions like contact tracing and venue check ins via the NHS Covid-19 app. For the public sector, our approach to managing risk has been challenged so that we can move faster, delivering urgent interventions and solutions in a more joined up way.

People have also been willing to share data, and collaborate more directly to help counter a very specific threat. This is a significant break from normal circumstances, where tasks and responsibilities such as governance, procurement, finance, and technology services would have been distributed across teams – and even different organisations – as an approach to risk management. The question is whether an organisation's tolerance of risk, especially around data sharing, can permanently change, or if they will inevitably return to more risk averse approaches.

3. National policy and local initiatives working more closely together

Traditionally, major changes to public policy have been top down, and built primarily around national initiatives. With this in mind, the first thing to note is that not all top down policy making is bad, especially when responding in a crisis. In an emergency situation like the pandemic there is a clear need for the government to act as part of a national response, offering the coordination and scale that local authorities can't.

However, top down structures and policy making in government have historically resulted in a lack of incentives and ability for civil servants, front line staff, and even communities themselves, to feed knowledge and lived experiences back to decision-makers. What we should be interested in is hearing from people who are closest to the real problems that need addressing, and who understand local context in ways that can help ensure national policy matches up with what needs to happen in reality.

During the pandemic, we witnessed time and time again the power of local communities who were ready to support services and central government interventions, plugging gaps and stepping in to help friends and neighbours – just getting things done to meet urgent needs. When this relationship was most effective it was because local feedback shaping policy and service decisions was genuine, listened to, and acted upon as part of national decision making.

The pandemic has highlighted that a more balanced and connected approach between national and local policy is needed, and the advantages of working more flexibly in this way, and with better feedback mechanisms in place. Stronger connections between citizens, services and the decisions made at a national level have the potential to significantly impact people's lives, delivering positive outcomes including community cohesion and the strengthening of society.

Everything can change

Digital and change initiatives no longer need to be seen as separate programmes, separate projects, or separate delivery priorities. Even before the pandemic, many of our public institutions were already moving beyond siloed digital programmes of work and a focus on transactional service delivery or digitisation. Instead, these organisations are focused on using digital and technology to change how their whole organisations work and how they create value. In doing so these places are better equipped to respond to both current and future change. They understand the importance of bringing delivery and policy closer together, and they can measure the impact of their work and how this improves people's lives.

This type of increasing and further reaching ambition for digital transformation is something we are now starting to see more widely, and is evidenced through the latest updated digital and technology strategies being published that look beyond Covid-19. For example, the DfE published its updated digital and technology strategy in April 2021. In it, Emma Stace, DfE's Chief Digital and Technology Officer, set out a departmental priority to bring policy and delivery closer together – an aim that was cemented by the forces of the pandemic and DfE's response to the crisis. As Emma explained in a blog post, "The coronavirus pandemic has led to digital and technology playing a much bigger role in how our department shapes its policy. We will continue to integrate policy with design and digital skills so that we can offer better services."[10]

When two plus two can equal five

What happens when something changes? The Covid-19 pandemic has made the immediate need for public services and policy more visible and urgent. It has been a universal experience, shared by our friends, families and colleagues, leading to new types of services and support, and collective responsibilities between national and local government, health services, and the voluntary and community sectors. When faced with significant change, and when responding to that change, we have seen that more is possible.

In this chapter we have explored the legacy of digital transformation, started to understand what we need to build on, and what we can learn from in our experiences before, and during the pandemic. We have considered how the public sector has been able to react faster, and adapt more rapidly to events and circumstances as they've evolved.

We have looked at opportunities to rethink our ambitions for digital transformation. Accepting that more impact is possible, the challenge is also to recognise that more impact is needed – now more than ever before – as we face new environmental and social challenges.

Next, we will look at the need for a hyper-local approach, creating greater benefits for people and their communities.

Multiplied Thinking: Key takeaways from chapter 1

- **Far greater impact is possible.** With modern ways of working, and through the use of design, technology and data, the impact and scale of our work can go far beyond what was previously thought to be achievable.

- **Focus on user outcomes.** Because impact is difficult to measure or quantify, focus on the one common thread that links everything together in the work of the public sector: people.

- **Make digital transformation work harder.** Learn from, and build on the experiences of what is now legacy digital transformation. Ask: what worked before, and why?

- **Move from digitisation, to digitalisation.** Focus on wholesale service transformation, dealing with constraints and organisational silos. Ensure that teams work towards service outcomes, understanding a broader set of needs within communities.

- **Learn from successful pandemic responses.** Recognise how whole organisations have been able to prioritise digital transformation, with new levels of tolerance towards managing risk, and with national policy and local initiatives working more closely together.

- **Everything can be more than the sum of its parts.** Anything becomes possible when something changes – whether that change is triggered by global events, or simply our own ability to make something happen.

2 Hyper-local futures

> "When people feel supported by strong human relationships, change happens. And when we design new systems that make this sort of collaboration and connection feel simple and easy, people want to join in."
>
> – Hillary Cottam[11]

In an age of globalisation, many of the major differences between the places we live have been diminished. That said, you can still find plenty of civic pride in the local and regional identities that have been shaped by economic, industrial and societal changes over time.

The places we live all continue to face specific challenges. These may be due to the legacy of their own particular geographical and historical contexts, but they are equally found in the effects of national and global events. Covid-19, for example, is a pandemic on a global scale, but it has been directly felt by individuals in every part of the UK.

The same can be said for policy decisions which are made at a national level, but which affect us all in individual and localised ways. Whenever we think about change, it's therefore important to focus on how it's experienced by people in their communities.

For services to respond better to individual and local situations, there is a need to create and maintain strong links between our institutions and communities – between the points at which policy is created and the places where people access services and support. This is also the opportunity for communities to shape services and policy decisions themselves, giving them a direct say in what happens.

Covid-19 has been a catastrophe on a scale most of us have never seen before. Yet the seriousness of the pandemic's challenges has been the catalyst for all kinds of change – both good and bad – and, increasingly, a new way to think about our local responses to meeting national and global challenges.

Global and local impact

The UK's NHS Test and Trace system was promised to be a "world beating" service. For a start, it had no shortage of taxpayer's money at its disposal. Its design and development was shaped by some of the most experienced consultants working in the field of design, technology and transformation, building upon established digital delivery approaches, as well as the service standards of the last decade.

However as reported regularly by the UK press, Test and Trace has only ever produced mixed, or to be less kind, extremely disappointing results. Based on Public Accounts Committee reports, it has also cost the UK taxpayer £37 billion so far . . .

So what went wrong? One thing that has become increasingly clear is that Test and Trace has worked far more effectively when it has relied on strong local links and has been delivered in partnership with local authorities.

Back in August 2020, BBC News reported how Blackburn with Darwen Council had created their own contact tracing system in which council staff used their local knowledge to track those individuals NHS Test and Trace couldn't find, often using the ability to send officers directly to people's addresses in order to reach them.[12] While the central system was tracing a relatively low 60% of people, this low tech local approach was successfully reaching up to 80% of others. Paul Fleming, Strategic Director of Resources at Blackburn, who helped to set up the local service, explained that it depended on good coordination, data management and oversight at the centre in order for the local authority to do what it is great at – working with communities. It was important for national and local systems to work together to fully understand local needs, while maintaining trust through the local people running established front line services.

Other councils across the country set up similar local approaches. When this worked well, it allowed local authorities to focus on the hard to reach cases, with the central system continuing to deal with the more numerous, common and more easily outsourced scenarios. The importance of this relationship was demonstrated again when it was reported that failures in the NHS Test and Trace programme helped fuel the spread of the Delta Covid-19 variant in Blackburn.[13] The central system failed to notify contact tracers in the Lancashire authority of 164 positive cases in late April and early May 2021, with the new variant subsequently gaining a strong foothold and infection rates surging in the North West of England.

In Blackburn's case, they only started to see more effective contact tracing once local connections were created and sustained through community knowledge and networks. When we talk about local connections, we mean any kind of mechanism through which policy or services can be delivered locally: it might include things like getting influential members of a community on board with initiatives, or bringing support directly to people's doors. Increasingly, this approach has become part of the UK's vaccination programme strategy. In a bid to encourage more people to get their jabs, vaccination buses have been used in places like Newcastle, where people have been unable to go to official vaccination centres, or where uptake has been lower.

As community champion Khaled Musharraf explained on the day a vaccination bus arrived in Elswick, "When people see the bus coming into the community, [the vaccine] becomes more open to them, they see it's more accessible – and it's the bus that is actually creating that connection. Some people were feeling hesitant [about getting the vaccine]. But the thing is, you can see how positive it is today – they are coming in".[14]

Areas like Elswick have been places that, historically, have experienced health inequalities and social deprivation. Trust built between authorities and communities becomes a key factor in such areas, with intervention requiring local knowledge, volunteers and coordination to get buy in from local people. At the same time, however, the vaccination bus wouldn't have been possible without the support of a national system providing the right data, medical equipment and training. The NHS staff may have been local, for instance, but the branded bus was part of a national government initiative. On this particular Sunday morning, with the support of community coordination, a further 150 people were reached and vaccinated.

As these examples show, to increase the reach and impact of services, it's essential to build trust with local people and harder to reach communities, while making the most of local knowledge, insight and connections.

A shift to working more closely with communities

In many ways, there's nothing new about the ideas we have explored so far. As far back as the 19th century, local government institutions were created in a way that gave them representation, accountability and a distinctly regional identity, so that they could meet the needs of their own local communities. Building on these origins, we have seen a continual growth in regional organising and collaboration in recent years, including political devolution, the creation of more mayoral authorities, and other initiatives seeking to empower local places.

It was back in September 2018, for example, when leaders from across the North of England first gathered together for a Convention of the North. This assembly had the aim of speaking with one clear voice on the need to rebalance the country's political focus.[15] While three years later, in 2021, the government committed to the political agenda of "levelling up" across the whole of the UK, "to ensure that no community is left behind, particularly as we recover from the Covid-19 pandemic".[16]

Citizen engagement

Councils have always played a vital role in local services, especially in how they maintain links to support across the voluntary and community sector. A more recent shift we can observe in the role of local government though is an increase in awareness of the need to involve citizens directly, putting people at the heart of decision making to seek better outcomes.

There has been a significant increase in things like citizens' assemblies being held across the UK, bringing together representatives of a community to deliberate a question and determine their response. In 2021 TPXimpact worked with Blackpool Council as they ran a climate assembly – a "mini Blackpool" of members who represented the demographics of the town. During the sessions, we heard from specialists in different aspects of the climate emergency and about action being taken both locally and elsewhere. The group then deliberated on what the council, local organisations and residents could do to tackle these issues. The assembly's prioritised recommendations formed a report which in turn has fed into the council's ongoing action plan.[17]

Why are things like this important? Because right now, every public institution in every town and city across the UK is facing incredibly tough decisions. How to "build back better" from a global pandemic; how to tackle a global climate emergency; and how to deal with an array of locally specific challenges, too.[18]

Taking on this work with citizens and other organisations can achieve four things:

1. **Social cohesion:** It improves the relationship between local authorities and citizens, by bringing people together to think through solutions to tough issues. This reduces the sense people often have of things being "done to" them and helps build social cohesion.
2. **New ideas:** It generates new ideas with higher levels of ambition. When there's a range of different perspectives, solutions can be explored that simply wouldn't be thought of within organisation or departmental silos.
3. **Sustained collaboration:** It generates sustained collaboration for delivering solutions. A large number of those who take part in deliberative processes, in places like Blackpool, tell us that they'd like to stay involved. For many, it's their first experience engaging with their council or other levels of government.
4. **Shared responsibility:** Getting citizen buy in through the co-design of solutions gives everyone a part to play, which can ease the amount of direct investment our public institutions need to make in solutions, helping us to do more where resources are limited. This is especially valuable with complex challenges like climate change, as responding at the scale required needs everybody, everywhere, to act.

Any efforts to work collaboratively with local communities and citizens must place inclusion at the centre. In the climate assembly in Blackpool, we were mindful of accessibility issues, with the whole process run online during lockdown, in a community where the adult reading age is below the national average. We therefore invested time in one to one support for participants ahead of and during the assembly sessions, and made sure the resources provided would be accessible to all.

Although the decision to run these sessions online was made due to the pandemic, we found that technology actually opened up participation to busy professionals and those with caring responsibilities, removing travel and distance as barriers to people getting involved. It also had the secondary benefit of providing some of the assembly members with confidence in using technology to speak with loved ones in lockdown.

This type of shift to working more closely with communities has the potential to lead to better solutions that are more likely to stand the test of time, as they are embedded within local places from the very start. As described by one Blackpool assembly member to our team, this approach has changed their own relationship with their community and what they now see is possible: "I started really looking forward to Tuesday evenings. I'm not someone who talks a lot, I like to use my eyes and ears, but when I wanted to contribute, I was able to."[19]

Investment in participation

Local participation is a multiplier. To deliver greater benefits for communities we must engage and work with people directly, as early as possible, and as often as we can. This requires a willingness from both the public sector and citizens to act together, investing in local ideas, as well as in places that bring people together like libraries, sports clubs and community hubs.

Experience has shown us that this type of work gets the best results, including how we build strong links between citizen engagement and digital transformation. It does, however, require time and investment. We know that local authorities are, and will continue to be, under financial pressure, and understand that there are critical staffing and funding constraints in the health system. But putting citizens' lived experience and voices at the heart of change leads to better outcomes. This may not always be easy, but it's certainly more cost effective than inaccurate, assumption based service delivery which may need to be undone and redone time and again.

In a world where resources are stretched, unlocking the potential of local communities and seeking their time, ideas, and direct engagement can help everyone to do more, with greater and lasting impact.

The Wigan Deal

One of the best examples of impact through this type of community participation is The Wigan Deal. Faced with significant austerity budget cuts in 2010, Wigan Council's leadership needed a new approach in order to continue providing services to the local community. They developed The Deal – an informal agreement between the council and everyone who lives or works in Wigan to create a better borough together.[20]

The Deal was launched on the council website and promoted through local campaigns and community networks. It clearly sets out roles and responsibilities for both the council – "Our Part", and local residents – "Your Part". For example, where the council promises to "keep your Council Tax as one of the lowest", the expectation of residents is that they "recycle more, recycle right". As the council says on its website, "we believe we can continue to balance our books if you help by doing things like recycling more, volunteering in your communities and using online services."[21]

For the council, The Deal's main objectives are to manage costs and service demand while improving the lives of residents. For local residents, The Deal gives them an important role to play in shaping the prospects of their own communities. This has been successful in many ways: Wigan Council has reduced its expenses, while improving services and health outcomes for citizens. There are now a number of Deals focused on different parts of the community in Wigan. The Deal for Business, for example, has encouraged businesses to hire locally and invest in their community, with the council then providing training for local people to meet business needs. By acting together with the community, the council has saved £115 million, and now has the second lowest council tax rates in Greater Manchester.

The Wigan Deal is a gold standard in citizen participation as it has improved social cohesion, increased shared responsibility, and is sustaining community collaboration in ways that continue to support improved local outcomes.

Hyper-local futures

When looking at what we can learn from the Covid-19 pandemic, it's important to recognise that this is a global event. Nevertheless, its effects are being felt locally, by individuals in communities all around the world.

With ongoing globalisation, and in the context of a progressively disrupted climate, issues at a global scale will increasingly shape how we live our day to day lives. It is happening already, with migration, climate change and pollution all global issues that are reaching further into our communities, influencing things like the availability of housing, the supply of goods and services, and the way authorities plan for disaster response.

The nature of these challenges compounds the need to create strong links back into local communities, giving people a way to be part of much needed change. It's worth noting that "local" can still mean large – it might equally apply to a whole region as a single town or city – but it implies those people who experience the impact of public policy and services in the places they live. It is a reminder that we should never lose sight of the people in society in the way we understand and deliver services and solutions.

Within the public sector, knowing more about the needs of a region, a city or even parts of a community within that place offers clear advantages. Targeted local responses to events and individual circumstances stand a greater chance of delivering more impact, often much more quickly. The ability to create and sustain these strong links to places to meet their specific needs goes beyond local. It enters the realm of what can be described as "hyper-local."

Hyper-local is a focus on the needs people have within a specific place or situation. This is the potential for solutions to be flexible and tailored around individual circumstances and local contexts. As we highlighted in examples like the NHS Test and Trace system, national policies and responses require investment to build trust and increase reach into communities. We can continue to deliver more impact by working towards more tailored approaches that are both co-created, supported and delivered at a local level.

This is the flexibility to meet everyone's needs within their own situation, considering their context, requirements and preferences. It is also a way of extending both the reach and effectiveness of services to everyone. By designing future solutions in this way we can create better outcomes for more people, enabling them to access services and support how and where they need to.

Strong community links

Hyper-local isn't a new idea, and is something that will already be familiar to many within the public sector. Following their responses to the pandemic, the challenge is now for policy makers and leaders to maintain support for the strong links they have built with communities and the help that has been provided by grassroots organisations.

Steve Butterworth, CEO of Neighbourly – a platform that helps businesses make a positive impact in their communities by donating volunteer time – explained it this way in June 2020: "While there will be a temptation to build something new as a pandemic recovery response, there is already a multitude of hyper-local causes working day in, day out to deliver food and other essential support. They know the people in their community on a named basis and have proved their ability to deliver over the last 12 weeks. We need to keep that lifeline alive."[22]

Nowhere has this been more true than in parts of the country that already had effective town or parish councils. Where funding is extremely tight, such councils are used to mobilising others rather than having to provide resources themselves.

In the pandemic, Harpenden Town Council collaborated with mutual aid groups to provide support to people in the area. They asked a local charity to provide a telephone helpline and worked with a local food bank to arrange a no questions asked food delivery service, with street coordinators arranging food bank collections. Known as Harpenden Cares, this support service still continues, and the relationships established in the town and even across individual streets have been greatly strengthened.[23]

Expecting difference to improve outcomes

Hyper-local approaches mean that we should expect differences in the solutions that work in one place or scenario, compared to what works in a different context or set of circumstances. It is important to consider how local solutions based on citizen needs must vary from place to place if they are to lead towards more impact and improved outcomes.

Difference can also represent lots of approaches in a single place. In one local government example, Leeds City Council has commissioned all of its 37 neighbourhood networks to tackle social isolation and loneliness, with each area providing a range of support to help people stay connected.[24] The key thing is that every area works and is funded independently, tailoring its approaches to local people around a hyper-local view of community assets and needs.

For example, one particular area might operate a theatre club due to its good access to bus routes into the city centre, while another area might focus on providing fitness classes. These different offers and support meet the needs of different age demographics and bring different communities together in new ways – helping to build community cohesion.

The success of this type of hyper-local approach shows that decision makers higher up in government, and especially those in charge of funding, need to accept more variation and localism within solutions in order to get the best possible outcomes.

Sharing knowledge is also key here. Places like Leeds have built strong networks that bring together learning across different areas, and what works in different contexts. This allows for differences, whilst also ensuring that approaches are joined up, and that each area has the potential to learn from what others are doing.

Hyper-local is a multiplier. As we saw with extending the reach of the UK vaccination programme, there is a need for joined up national infrastructure, and links to national policy, but we have to create flexibility through local initiatives, instead of simply applying a standardised template that might not work as intended for the different needs of specific areas and communities.

Increasing political engagement with local communities

As we saw with Blackpool's climate assembly, a hyper-local approach also offers greater opportunities for organisational and political leaders to engage directly with the communities they serve and represent. This is a key piece of the puzzle when it comes to delivering more impact, as leaders need the right mechanisms to first discover, and then meet, people's needs. Importantly, it helps these individuals and groups make tough decisions on local challenges together.

Strengthening local political engagement is a central part of the Towns Fund, a £3.6 billion central government investment into over a hundred towns in England, and a focus of work TPXimpact have been part of since 2020.[25]

Under this initiative, funding is being applied differently from place to place according to local priorities, from the regeneration of high streets to investment in skills to support more local jobs. As part of the investment process, community connectors – people with trusted local networks and knowledge – have been piloted to help towns build longer term relationships with their communities, businesses and other funding partners. Working collaboratively with leaders and investors, each place has built on its strong local links, creating a long term plan for sustainable change that will shape its future.

The Towns Fund has been a timely reminder that every local town and area has its own unique strengths and opportunities linked to industry, business, the scale of local ambition and, most of all, its people. While it's a significant programme of work that comes from national government investment, the true strength of the programme is in how these unique local links have been part of the response.

As the Towns Fund demonstrates, hyper-local approaches can create and sustain meaningful links between real lived experiences, and policy, structures and decision making processes. With hyper-local, we can achieve impact that is felt in a much more meaningful and personal way as it connects with, and becomes part of, people's everyday lives. This will be important to our ongoing response to Covid-19, but beyond that, it will shape how our lives are affected by future forces of disruption and change.

Preparing for future disruption

The Covid-19 pandemic has demonstrated that it's possible for the public sector to face up to immediate and complex changing situations. But as the climate emergency shows, instead of looking at the pandemic as an isolated incident we should be prepared to face increasing global disruption. Rising sea levels and unpredictable weather patterns now seem inevitable, even though the knock on effects of these events are not easy to predict or fully understand.

Since we started burning fossil fuels on a large scale around 150 years ago, there has been an average global temperature increase of a little more than 1 degree Celsius causing major public health, environmental and economic issues around the world.[26] At the 26th Conference of the Parties (COP26) climate change conference in November 2021, leaders committed to limiting further warming, in line with a promise to cap temperatures to 1.5 degrees above pre Industrial levels. Reflecting on the task ahead, COP26 President Alok Sharma said: "We can now say with credibility that we have kept 1.5 degrees alive. But, its pulse is weak and it will only survive if we keep our promises and translate commitments into rapid action."[27] To make progress we now require rapid, far reaching and unprecedented changes in all aspects of society.[28]

Taking radical action

The seriousness of the situation cannot be overstated, but it's important to recognise that even with the severity of the climate emergency, change is possible. If you need convincing of this point then consider the types of radical action that have taken place in response to Covid-19.

In order to act before it's too late, we need to radically change how we use transport, create clean, healthier air for people to breathe, and reduce the level of household and business emissions that contribute to global warming. We have already seen that local authorities are capable of taking this kind of action, with councils such as Royal Greenwich instantly shutting busy inner city roads and widening pedestrian areas in 2020 to encourage walking and cycling.[29] Even though this was done to create space for social distancing, and not as a first step to dealing with climate change, it shows that the rapid altering of public infrastructure and transport systems is possible when there's the will to do so.

The question is how we create and sustain the additional willpower needed for more radical action in the face of increasing global disruption. We can't afford to wait on lengthy consultations before we're willing to close roads again and build more cycling infrastructure. And even then, it won't be enough.

We face the very real risk of losing any ability we have found to take faster and more decisive action for the health of our communities, even before we start to consider how to take more radical steps in future. There are already examples elsewhere in London where plans to continue to reduce traffic and limit people's dependence on cars have sparked bitter conflict and where legal challenges are currently escalating. There's a danger that many of the experiments put in place during the pandemic will be shut down before we fully realise their benefits for society – with temporary cycle ways and extended pedestrian areas already being put back to pre pandemic layouts.

Decisions will have to be made as to how we eventually build back better from the pandemic while still moving towards climate change goals. It would be far more straightforward and timely – not to mention cost effective – to have all these tough conversations at the same time. Whatever the approach taken, it's vital that people's lived experiences are at the heart of such decisions. For any of these changes to stick they have to bring together the work of our public institutions with the interests, needs, and ideas of businesses and people in local communities. The best chance of success comes from a hyper-local approach.

Change built from local collaboration and connection

In this chapter we have looked at how strong local links are needed to deliver more impact, with collaboration and service delivery that brings together national policy, central planning, and local coordination. While we have seen increased community power and participation in action, this now has to be for the long term, as we know that we will need to do more in response to continuing and future disruption, including the climate emergency.

With a hyper-local focus, and through investment in work with local communities, we can deliver better outcomes. There is also the potential for increased political engagement that brings together national and local leaders such as with the Towns Fund.

However, although there's a strong argument that many organisations are starting to see the value of this type of work, many don't know where to start in supporting and sustaining these approaches in how they work for the long term. What is clear is that we must sustain the types of radical action we have seen in how different local areas have responded to the pandemic.

Next, we will look at the role that our public institutions need to play in delivering more impact, and sustaining these changes in ways that can meet future challenges.

Multiplied Thinking: Key takeaways from chapter 2

- **Recognise the importance of local connections.** Increase the reach and impact of services by building trust with local people and harder to reach communities. Make the most of local knowledge, insight and connections.

- **Put citizens' lived experience at the heart of change.** Work more closely with communities to increase social cohesion, generate new ideas with higher levels of ambition and create shared responsibilities.

- **Invest in participation.** Engage and work with people directly, as early as possible, and as often as you can. Use collaboration to help the public sector achieve more, even when resources are scarce.

- **Adopt hyper-local approaches.** Focus on the needs people have within specific places or situations to deliver improved outcomes. Solutions can then be designed to adapt to different local contexts.

- **Strengthen political engagement.** Invest in work that creates and sustains meaningful links between real lived experiences and policy, structures and decision making processes.

- **Sustain radical action.** Build on the rapid responses and change that has been made possible during the pandemic. Doing more to sustain and support this type of action as we face the climate emergency and other future challenges.

3 Models of the world we want to build

"The organisations that we build must be models of the world we want to create."

— *Umair Haque*[30]

The public sector is at the heart of society. We will all come into contact with, or depend upon public services at key points in our lives, whether through local or central government, or the strong links many services have into the third sector and the voluntary and community sectors. From large national charities to local community based initiatives, and from central government departments to local NHS Trusts, the way each organisation works, and how the public sector works together, shapes how we all experience key events in our lives.

In response to Covid-19, our public institutions have had to make rapid adjustments to their ways of working. We are now at an important point of reflection as our organisations start to look ahead and think beyond the pandemic, and about how they might need to work in the future.

As the writer Umair Haque explains in the quote at the start of this chapter, we have the opportunity to shape our world through the kinds of organisations we create. If we imagine the kind of world we want to be part of, and the outcomes we want to help shape for people and society, we can then build our organisations in ways that will bring about this change.

If we want increased flexibility to meet individual and changing needs in new ways, delivering joined up services with more openness and transparency, and greater equality and inclusion, then we must design our organisations to reflect these priorities. This is the link between how we work and the results of what we do, making it possible to deliver far greater impact together.

The reshaping of our public institutions

Due to the pandemic, every organisation now has some level of remote working, with a particular focus on video conferencing and virtual meeting solutions. In theory this has given people more flexibility than ever before around how and when they work, supported by new tools and devices.

However, many of our organisations and teams still lack the flexibility they need to work in new ways. Even with new digital tools, processes remain the same, as do team and management structures, the way issues are resolved or escalated, and how caseloads and tasks are managed. In the worst scenarios organisations have simply moved meetings and workflows online, leading to reports of Zoom fatigue, and people spending all day on back to back video calls.

Digital transformation isn't just the ability to do Zoom calls or to hold remote staff meetings, it's about making fundamental changes to systems and processes. The shift we have seen in working patterns hasn't always considered the best way to make use of new tools and technologies, with instant messaging and the power of other collaborative approaches often overlooked. This includes giving people the permission where needed to work more independently and more asynchronously.

The lack of change to how we work continues to be influenced by existing office culture, with middle managers often using video calls as a means to maintain visibility of people and their work. This represents a lack of trust, reinforced by hierarchical structures that don't give teams and individuals the autonomy to make decisions independently, or to set their own priorities aligned to shared goals.

Everything we're describing is the result of organisations and teams not stopping to think about alternative approaches to how they organise their work. In the end it means our business models and uses of technology are not fit for purpose.

Agile organisations, not agile projects

The public sector has increasingly adopted agile principles to support technology and service delivery. This approach has been a key part of digital transformation for more than a decade of investment in programmes across central government, local government, and health.

Agile is a method of delivering work known for its flexibility and adaptability. It dictates a team's rhythms and ways of working, and also influences culture, fostering an environment of trust and transparency. Most importantly, it allows teams to learn from their work and make adjustments as they go along, also known as working iteratively.

As the GOV.UK service manual explains, agile delivery is an alternative to the traditional waterfall delivery methods used in IT and software delivery: "With waterfall methods the process is sequential. You start by gathering requirements, making plans and going through procurement processes. You then design the product and build it. In the final stage you test and release it to the public. It's only at this end stage that you get feedback and find out if it works for your users . . . Agile takes a different approach. You do all these things – gathering requirements, planning, designing, building and testing – at the same time."[31]

The core principles behind agile are set out in the Agile Manifesto, which was first published in 2001. In this now established delivery model for digital projects in government, teams are required to demonstrate value continuously, with a user centred focus to ensure that solutions meet user needs. This has required a significant mindset shift in how organisations manage risk, encouraging teams to start small, and to deliver solutions in incremental stages.

Beyond individual agile digital transformation initiatives, what we have seen more than ever since the start of the Covid-19 pandemic is the need for agile organisations. What we now need to focus on is creating organisations that are more capable of adapting to change.

Many of our public institutions find this extremely difficult. As an example of how we are failing to adapt, some of the most pressing challenges the public sector now faces are service backlogs, which continue to grow in size. The Institute for Fiscal Studies reported in August 2021, for example, that since the start of the pandemic, the number of people waiting for NHS treatment in England had grown by a fifth.[32]

Why are backlogs in health still increasing? This is clearly a complex question to answer. But we suggest it's at least in part because existing processes and systems are simply too rigid to cope with change. While staff might be available, the systems they work with can't support any substantial changes to existing models of delivery. With services not able to operate as they were originally designed due to the continuing effect of Covid-19 restrictions, there's little flexibility to deal with increasing levels of service demand, even with promises of more funding, improved technology, or increases in staff numbers.

Defining the modern public institution

The economist Milton Friedman famously said that: "Only a crisis – actual or perceived – produces real change."[33] As we start to look beyond the public sector's response to Covid-19 we have the opportunity to reimagine our organisations. To do this we will need to find ways to step outside existing constraints. This means exploring new models that will create more flexibility to respond, and keep responding to change. But defining what makes a modern organisation in the public sector is difficult.

It is common for digital transformation programmes to talk about creating 21st century organisations, but we should challenge this. We are already nearly a quarter of the way through this century and some parts of the public sector still don't look significantly different in 2022 compared to 2002.

Technology and digital change have clearly shaped our organisations during this time. However, the 21st century doesn't just demand new digital tools and ways of delivering services. It demands new business models, new ways of organising, and more agile, responsive approaches. To create truly agile organisations, we will need to see a realignment of our value systems, individual behaviours, and fundamentally, how people organise and work together in a trusted and empowered way.

This is also about recognising that the world has changed and now demands a different type of response. At the 2021 Solace Summit (Britain's largest gathering of public sector and local government professionals) Chris Naylor, Chief Executive of the London Borough of Dagenham opened a panel discussion by saying that: "it feels like a pivotal moment for both public policy and leadership . . . existential threats like climate change, changes in technology and global pandemics feel less existential today . . . they are, if anything, the new normal."[34]

Following Covid-19 and the climate crisis, this has to be the decade where we reshape our public institutions for the next generation. In the 1920s we saw a major shift of culture in society across the Western world with nations experiencing rapid industrial and economic growth, with renewed hope for change. What if the 2020s could represent a radical shift in how our public institutions reshape society for the next generation?

New models of the world

As we now look ahead, the challenge we face is to create organisations capable of responding to change. This means purposefully structuring what we do internally to enable us to meaningfully shape and influence the complex reality of the world outside.

To achieve this, organisations will need to be digitally enabled, with an increased focus on how they organise around policy and service outcomes. They will require diverse teams and thinking, and the support of agile governance processes, and open, collaborative ways of working to succeed. Teams will need increased autonomy to make decisions, and the ability to design and manage how services are created and delivered. But most of all, they will be able to move away from traditional business structures and management hierarchies.

Organisations aligned around purpose

What we are proposing is that all parts of the public sector organise in new ways. This immediately feels like a significant challenge with the complexity and size of many of the organisations involved. But we can start by anchoring everything an organisation does to purpose.

Purpose is the reason something exists, or the reason why something is done or created. In the case of public sector organisations, purpose should be clearly linked to the policy and services they deliver. We already see this now: government departments have clear remits around areas of policy they're responsible for; the health sector has the NHS Charter setting out its commitments to patients; and in the third sector, most organisations have clear, shared goals. This is sometimes described as a mission, with Crisis dedicated to "ending homelessness", for example, and Cancer Research UK aiming to "bring forward the day when all cancers are cured".

The importance of purpose is this. No successful business ever starts with an organisational structure. As the author Nassim Nicholas Taleb explains, "business plans and funding work backwards".[35] By this he is referring to the fact that most big business success stories (such as Microsoft, Apple and Google) started organically. They grew as the result of people being invested in solving specific problems, with a clear purpose. Their initial success at least was more through shared values and mission as it was a business plan. The planning, structures and operationalising that has enabled these businesses to grow can all be tracked back to alignment around purpose.

Despite this, a problem in many modern businesses is that purpose has become widely associated with corporate brand positioning. As consumers have become increasingly aware of social and environmental issues, many organisations have begun to talk freely about purposeful business as a way of demonstrating positive ethical credentials. Often these claims are unsubstantiated, or an afterthought to usual business operations. This has led to a dilution of what it means for a business to align what it does around its purpose, which should instead sit at the heart of how everyone in an organisation works together, organising around a shared and clearly defined mission.

The biggest challenge organisations face is how to reach this point of shared understanding, where every individual and team is truly invested in their work in this way. As an example of the scale of the challenge, Harvard Business Review reported on research with 20 major corporations in Australia which highlighted that just 29% of employees answered correctly when asked to identify their employer's long term strategy from among six choices.[36]

This data isn't a surprise and most probably reflects how many staff members are disconnected with the corporate use of purpose as their companies use this to position and present a desired public face to the rest of the world. However, to be fully aligned around purpose, we need to look more carefully at how our organisations move into action and mobilise their teams.

From purpose to vision

The best way for people to have a shared sense of purpose is for them to work together towards a suitably ambitious goal. This is why we need vision.

Vision is how we can move from purpose into action. It gives us a model for doing – the process of clearly describing and setting out what we are working towards.

If you have ever been involved with digital transformation programmes, you may have spent time defining a vision, or co-creating a vision statement with your organisation. Many senior leadership teams invest in this work, but the results are often generic, and ultimately, not very useful.

A useful vision statement describes an ideal end state that we can work towards. It's a description of a future scenario that starts to ask the right questions – giving teams problems to solve, and ways to measure progress.[37] It should also be bold because it offers us an alternative to how things exist now. Vision can work on a number of levels, representing change being worked towards in a region or city, including economic, work and health outcomes, or describing an ideal future state for services like Adult Social Care. It could even be a future policy to transform something like a regional transport system.

Where there has been a bold, ambitious, vision, parts of the public sector have already successfully regenerated local areas – reimagining services, and changing lives. One such initiative is Digital Salford, set up and run by the Salford Council in collaboration with key stakeholders, including the local NHS Trust, University, and the private sector including MediaCityUK. Responsible for a number of new initiatives, Digital Salford aims to promote positive social impact for citizens through digital enablement, innovation, inward investment and smart city technology for citizen welfare.

Early on, the council's digital transformation team, led by Steven Fry, Chief Digital Officer, worked with its partners to design and agree a vision for Digital Salford: "To make Salford the most attractive city for digital enterprise and to establish Salford as a leading digital economy AND in doing so, to ensure that innovation and growth is directly connected to outcomes for Salford people."[38]

This is a vision clearly aligned to purpose. It has helped to shape and influence the investments made in creating improved outcomes for local people. As an example of an early initiative, in 2018 the council launched Digital You, working with community organisations to support almost 8,000 residents over two years. A key part of their vision to create a better, fairer Salford, Digital You is focused on improving digital literacy to tackle issues such as social isolation which helps improve health and wellbeing and enables people access to learning and job opportunities.

This is also a hyper-local approach, with initiatives connected into the local community as well as local business. As Steven Fry explains: "We have been creating a social movement for change by involving stakeholders from the public, voluntary and private sectors . . . We have been able to highlight where organisations, across sectors, can demonstrate their corporate social responsibility by supporting the movement to increase digital inclusion."[39]

Changing the story

In her book *Fear Less*, Dr Pippa Grange, a leading sports psychiatrist, explains that "we build our identity and our beliefs about what's possible on the back of stories we take as true." Stories are the ideas we have accepted, about ourselves, and the way things are around us. As Dr Pippa goes on to explain, the important thing is that we can control our stories, even when we can't control the circumstances.[40]

Our circumstances in the public sector mean dealing with a range of difficult constraints. This is everything from politics and power dynamics, to how we deal with legacy technology and the operational risks attached to services that millions of people need to access. But the opportunity is to create a new story, a shared vision that enables us to work within these constraints. To change what our organisations are capable of, we need better stories to shape what people collectively believe is possible.

As Digital Salford demonstrates, the importance of having a clearly articulated shared vision is actually about the power of storytelling. Stories are what connect the here and now with the future. Through any work to design and share a new vision we are setting out possible futures that underpin our goals and ambitions, and with the right investment we can then make the changes we're describing a reality.

For new ideas to succeed we also need to harness the collective energy and ambitions of communities. As with our Salford example, public institutions must empower people to take ownership of their stories, giving voices to communities, rather than being a single voice or storyteller themselves. As Rob Hopkins, the founder of the Transition Movement, explains in his book *From What Is to What If*, it is when communities come together to start telling new stories about what their future could be – the potential of their collective imagination – that we can find exciting possibilities.[41]

2020 vision

It is worth saying at this point that the vision we collectively set out and work towards often turns out to be wrong. To take one obvious example, 2020 was the focal point of many digital transformation vision statements and roadmaps, but no one could have predicted what actually happened that year. As we now see the public sector setting out 2030 plans, we have to understand that although these are useful, they need to be flexible to change and future opportunities. It doesn't matter if we will need to make adjustments as we go. Stories can be retold, evolving over time as they're shared. This gives us the ability to respond to change if we're open to new possibilities.

Finally, it's important that stories enable us to work beyond existing organisational forms and structures. Not only is there an opportunity to reimagine how departments and systems like health are organised. Instead, we can imagine a world where public institutions take distinctly different forms, or where there are completely new ways for organisations to interconnect and work together. This will mean acting out our values, and applying principles that shape what we will and won't do – making more ambitious models of the world possible.

Transparency and working in the open

In setting out the new models of the world we want to build, we have to be able to communicate our vision, bringing everyone on board with new ways of organising and working. A key part of this process is building trust, with the need for increased transparency both inside and outside our organisations.

We can think about an organisation as the house we build for ourselves and our teams to work from. The windows we build into our work are about giving ourselves a way to connect with the world outside, as well as letting the world see us.[42] When organising and aligning work around purpose and vision we need transparency to keep ourselves accountable, and by opening up our work we also benefit from external feedback, new perspectives and the ability to build on the work of others.

There have been different patterns of sharing during the pandemic. This has highlighted both the positives of working in the open, and the results of keeping the front door to your organisation firmly closed to the outside world. As Matt Jukes from TPXimpact explains, a lack of transparency makes it very difficult for organisations to build trust, and in the context of Covid-19 this had wide reaching consequences: "Some individuals took [working in the open during the pandemic] on themselves where official channels were lacking – this was a true public service but a burden that I believe should have been shared and better supported. Unfortunately much of the higher profile work was tight lipped and formal in its communications – and all the worse for it when issues emerged. The amount of conspiracy theories that filled the space of open communication was notable in 2020."[43]

Transparency and working in the open is a multiplier. Just like Salford, more organisations are now taking advantage of its effects by publicly sharing their vision and strategy. Another good example is Royal Greenwich Council who published their first digital strategy in November 2020 with a public commitment to working in the open. As Kit Collingwood, Assistant Director for Digital and Customer Services explained, making the strategy transparent and open for comment from the public was a new way of working for Royal Greenwich, but was designed to make them accountable for running the best council possible. An important part of this change was also the leadership of the council's Chief Executive, and the Leader of the Council, who supported this high level of openness alongside the council's bold ambitions for digital transformation.[44]

More of the public sector has to now be willing to collectively open up its work in this way, creating transparency with both the public, and each other, as we seek to deliver a more ambitious vision for how our organisations shape the world around us.

New ways of organising

As we have seen time and time again, teams and organisations are more than the sum of their parts, with individuals aligned around shared goals able to deliver impressive results. The question is how to organise to make the best use of the skills, experience, knowledge, energy and focus that each individual brings to their work.

Organising models are always there if you are willing to look hard enough. These models are commonly our default settings, based on how things have always worked, or how businesses were designed to function in a different era.

Many organising models which determine how our businesses function in reality are both:

- **Internally focused:** These models start with the needs of the organisation, rather than the needs of service users or citizens. As a consequence, business activities are most dependent on internal perspectives and business as usual priorities. This leads to the reinforcement of existing decision making rather than the ability to challenge existing structures and hierarchies. People (HR), technology (IT departments), policy and delivery functions mostly work separately under layers of management to solve what are determined to be business problems.
- **Technology-oriented:** This is the extension of internally focused businesses. It is when the way an organisation works is determined by its technology and system choices, and the constraints in place due to the way IT systems have been set up and must be maintained.

These approaches, along with how they shape team structures and ways of working, limit the reach and impact of the services our organisations are able to deliver. At their worst, they focus on what's best for maintaining systems and existing team structures, over what needs to happen to create the greatest benefits, improving outcomes for citizens and society.

So what's the alternative? When it comes to how we organise to increase impact, we increasingly need what we can describe as a **service-oriented** approach: starting with user needs, and being prepared to align all internal business activities to support improved service outcomes.

Service organisations

In the public sector the idea of truly organising everything an organisation does around user needs and outcomes is still radical. Although we're now used to starting with user needs in our digital programmes, this isn't reflected in most of the sector's approach to organisation design.

When you look at who was successful throughout the pandemic, it was not those operating with traditional business processes and organising models, but instead, agile businesses like Amazon which already had digital first infrastructure. They represent the type of modern organisations that understand the importance of building everything – infrastructure, technology, ways of working – around a clear customer value proposition.

In the same way, any public sector organisation that intends to meet user expectations needs to collectively focus everything it does on service outcomes. This is the idea of service organisations.[45]

In chapter 1 we introduced the idea of moving to the wholesale redesign of services, thinking beyond individual digital interactions in isolation. This work must include the design of services both frontstage and backstage. Not only is it important that we design how the user experience or frontstage of a service works (the part customers or end users experience directly), we must also design how the service is operationalised. To use a simple analogy, what is experienced in the restaurant by customers (frontstage), is ultimately determined by how well the kitchen runs (backstage).

Service organisations are multipliers. What we are describing is a process of change that is achieved by looking outwards. Where an organisation will optimise and plan its internal functions, organising its capabilities around what needs to happen externally.

Instead of relying on separate interfaces between siloed products and services to determine business structures, teams, technology and systems, service organisations design everything and everyone's work around user outcomes. This means people work increasingly with shared goals, rather than in traditional functional silos.

This also links back to the importance of purpose and vision. A clear and ambitious vision aligned to purpose is how teams then prioritise their work to support change in the most meaningful way. With new organising models each function or team has clear accountabilities for enabling the organisation to succeed in its overall objectives. They are empowered to make decisions that will bring about these aims as effectively as possible.

Changes to the shape and autonomy of teams

To create a service organisation requires an increasing alignment of teams in policy, operations and digital. When we look at the legacy of digital transformation one failure we have already highlighted is the continued separation of these functions. Frameworks like the DDaT (Digital, Data, and Technology) profession in government continue to reinforce this by not recognising policy as part of delivery alongside digital specialists.

Service organisations need to give teams autonomy and account-ability for the service outcomes in the policy areas they work with. Put into action this means setting department strategies where policy direction and delivery work is aligned around shared goals.

The Department for Education (DfE) is one department that has clearly set out this ambition for policy and digital teams to work together, and there is already a User Centred Policy Design team estab-lished at the Ministry of Justice. Emphasising the importance of this change to how teams are organised and funded in May 2021, James Reeve, Head Of Digital at DfE, explained that: "We already have lots of teams, but constant change has led to a weakening of their purpose. So we'd like to recommit them to solving particular problems for our users. This means setting up long lived multidisciplinary teams in each area of work with a strong mission."[46]

There is increasing talk of this type of investment in long lived teams across the public sector. This is the shift from funding projects to funding teams of specialists. In practice it should mean teams stay together to not only build a service, but to run, scale, and continue to improve it.

This is how we enable our teams to become multipliers – with people able to deliver far greater impact when working with shared goals and values. It is essential that we now continue to empower the people in our organisations to do more through how they are organised, and how work is funded.

Prepared for change

We said earlier that some businesses were more able to adapt during the pandemic as they were already organising themselves internally around a clear customer value proposition. But it wasn't just parts of the private sector that were prepared for change, with fast and effective responses also coming from many organisations providing public services and support. The most successful were already well on their way to adopting digital first models, with increasingly service-oriented approaches shaping how they work.

Parkinson's UK is one such organisation. Founded with a clear purpose to "find a cure, and improve life for everybody affected by Parkinson's", it supports more than 145,000 people in the UK living with the condition, with this number set to dramatically increase in the coming years.[47]

In 2019 the Service Transformation Team set out the challenge ahead: "Our direct services, providing support to thousands of people and their loved ones across the UK, are unable to scale to reach this demand. We're already struggling to be there for everyone that needs us. Alongside this, we know the world is changing. User expectations and behaviours are changing and people are looking for support in different ways."[48]

Since this point, the team has embedded new skills and approaches including user research, service design and agile ways of working. Through an ambitious digital change programme they have also created Parkinson's Connect – a new support service that makes the best use of technology to meet the needs of people with Parkinson's, and their family, friends, and carers.[49]

Parkinson's Connect was designed around a new service blueprint that was co-created with the people the organisation seeks to support, helping them to understand and meet needs at different points of people's lives. Its aims include connecting with people when they are diagnosed; improving support for complex needs; providing personalised advice and information – both online and offline; and empowering people to live well with Parkinson's. For the first time, healthcare professionals can now refer people directly to Parkinson's Connect, and if you're newly diagnosed, the service now offers information through a Digital Health Assistant.[50]

When Covid-19 hit, Parkinson's UK was faced with the challenge of accelerating their move away from traditional telephone and face to face services to a fully digitally enabled model, and embedding remote ways of working into their culture for the longer term. Thanks to the digital transformation work already undertaken with Parkinson's Connect, the organisation knew how to build and scale new types of services that could continue to provide flexible support to individuals in the changing environment of the pandemic.

This example is the result of an organisation aligned around a mission to make a difference in people's lives. They have a shared story, where the effectiveness and reach of support is multiplied by new operating models and uses of technology. By the time of the pandemic, Parkinson's UK already understood the value of delivering value quickly, learning and experimenting and, most of all, of working closely with the people it supports. Moving away from traditional organising models, it's a service organisation in every sense.

Changing how we work and how we work together

In this chapter we have looked at how we organise. Not only is this about changing how we work, it's about changing how organisations can work together to have greater impact.

We started with the importance of aligning work with purpose and having a clear vision to work towards. We have seen how there is the opportunity to change the stories that shape what our organisations and communities believe is possible, in spite of the constraints and challenges we face.

We have also compared different organising models and what it means to be a service organisation, including how organisations like Parkinson's UK were already on this journey – showing how this was an important factor in their successful response to the pandemic.

Next, we will consider the change in mindset needed for our organisations to work in new ways and make more impact possible.

Multiplied Thinking: Key takeaways from chapter 3

- **Become an agile organisation.** Focus on being an agile organisation, not just delivering agile projects. With the right changes to how we organise people, teams and priorities, far more impact is possible.

- **Align activities around purpose and vision.** Move from purpose to action, being sure to harness the collective energy and ambitions of both organisations and communities.

- **Change the story.** Stories challenge our existing beliefs, and shape what people collectively believe is possible. Even if you can't change the circumstances, you can always change the story.

- **Work in the open.** Ensure that people can connect and collaborate outside of their immediate teams and with other organisations. Support teams to work transparently and to be accountable for the outcomes they deliver.

- **Organise in new ways.** Become a service organisation by organising internal business functions and capabilities around user outcomes to increase the impact of work externally.

- **Fund and prioritise long lived teams.** Invest in teams for the long term, ensuring that they stay together, to not only build services, but to run, scale, and continue to improve them.

4 A design state of mind

"In New York, concrete jungle where dreams are made of, there's nothing you can't do."[51]

– Jay-Z

For digital transformation to deliver more impact the public sector needs ways of ensuring that services go further in how they meet people's needs, and achieve the right outcomes. It also has to do this while recognising and being prepared to work with increasingly complex problems and systems.

If we are going to reshape our organisations to make this happen, the challenge is how we can individually and then collectively start to think and act differently.

The Covid-19 pandemic has already shown us that our organisations can do this. We have to be prepared to continue questioning how we work, and how our behaviours create and sustain the belief that more is possible. We need ways of responding quickly and decisively to future challenges while dealing with uncertainty and unknowns.

As we start to look beyond the pandemic, we also need teams that can apply new thinking to deliberately challenge and shape what happens next. This is at the heart of responding to change with increased ambition and a bold vision for what future services can achieve. With the right mindset, and by placing people at the centre of our work and decision making, we give ourselves the ability to increase the reach and impact of the next generation of public services.

New ways of thinking and doing

Our mindsets are shaped by the world around us. The places, people, and experiences we come into contact with in our everyday lives influence how we think, feel, and behave in any given situation – including how we respond to challenges in our work. But just as our environments shape our mindset, we can also shape our environments. We can influence what happens, helping to bring about new models of the world through our organisations.

For digital transformation to deliver more impact, the public sector must be prepared to respond differently through how we work both individually and collectively. This means challenging and resetting long standing behaviours and norms that define how our organisations work, reevaluating what we believe is possible.

In this chapter we will look more closely at what it means to adopt a design mindset. This brings together a number of ideas, but most importantly, it's about how we place people directly at the centre of our work, including all of the business, operational and decision making processes that shape what happens.

A design mindset is also about how we help people to become more effective at working together. Design gives us ways of working with complexity, reframing problems and exploring new ideas and opportunities. Combined with agile approaches like learning by doing, this is the best possible way of supporting teams to deliver better services and solutions while managing risk and uncertainty.

From design thinking to organisations that think differently

The idea of design mindsets originates from design thinking. This concept is attributed to the consultancy firm IDEO, who began to use it in the 1970s to describe the elements of design practices that are the most learnable and teachable – empathy, optimism, iteration, creative confidence, experimentation, and an embrace of ambiguity and failure.[52] The goal of design thinking is to create products that more closely align to people's needs and expectations, creating positive service experiences and innovating through user centred design approaches.

There are lots of ways design thinking can be put into practice. Most design teams will all work with some variation of largely similar approaches, and it's common to see teams adopting frameworks like the Design Council's Double Diamond which has become popular since its first introduction in 2005.[53] Design thinking has also shaped the agile delivery methods that are widely used across the public sector, including the user centred design approaches and roles found in digital teams. Following frameworks such as DDaT (Digital, Data, and Technology), teams now deploy a number of specialist design job roles and skill sets including interaction design, content design, service design, and user research.

However, even if we consider user centred design to be one of the successes of investment in digital transformation, in reality, many organisations are not user centred in how they operate. In delivery, it's still all too common for teams to use what are considered to be user centred approaches, but without truly thinking and acting in ways that question the effect their decisions have on improving real user outcomes. They may be conducting regular user research and working with design specialists, but the outputs of this work can still be rooted in business as usual and risk averse behaviours.

Beyond digital delivery teams, the real risk is that we also try to apply user centred approaches more widely in organisations that aren't able to think and act effectively in this way. This includes how teams are asked to prioritise work and implement policy, with the danger that any user centred work becomes no more than theatre – creating the impression that decisions are being shaped and directed in user centred ways, but while power and influence over what happens is controlled from elsewhere.

The challenge is now how the public sector moves from limited applications of user focus in projects, to shaping how entire organisations think and respond in more user centred ways. This is the need for all of our teams and functions to learn about what it means to adopt a design mindset.

Putting people at the centre of all our work

If we really want to deliver more meaningful impact and improved outcomes in people's lives, then all activities inside the public sector must be aligned to ensure that decision making places people at the centre of all processes, policy and design decisions.

As we set out, user centred design is already an established part of digital delivery. Yet, for digital transformation to deliver more impact, we now need to be far more radical in how we place and keep users at the centre of all our work. Otherwise, given the positions of power we hold as delivery teams or public servants, we risk placing ourselves at the centre of how problems are solved, working from our own perspectives of what other people need – including any assumptions and biases we might have.[54]

In contrast, we need more inclusive design and research processes, and the type of community engagement and hyper-local approaches first described in chapter 2. This means always looking to put other people's perspectives at the centre of our work, being prepared to really listen to real life experiences, and creating space for people to express how they're feeling and what they need. A design mindset is about continuously aligning work in this way.

What we don't want is any notion of "empathy" towards users becoming a cold debate in our teams, removed from the reality of people's lives. A good example of how to start to address this is exposure hours, an idea introduced by The Government Digital Service (GDS) in 2014 setting out that everyone in a delivery team should observe user research for at least two hours every six weeks.[55] This was subsequently extended across the entire organisation, including the Chief Executive, and it has also been adopted by digital leaders in parts of the NHS and elsewhere in the public sector. Set up effectively, and aligned to activities planned and run by research specialists, this kind of initiative might include people observing interviews or sessions where parts of services are tested with end users. This gives members of an organisation the opportunity to observe how people's lives are affected by the decisions they make and the types of interventions or solutions being delivered.

Although exposure hours can be effective, this still doesn't necessarily position service users at the centre of work. With a design mindset, the solution is to create even more time and space for our colleagues to participate in shared design processes as part of closer work with communities. Most of all, and even with investment in this type of approach, we need teams that are able to actively question where power and influence sits in decision making processes. This is how we ensure we are listening to the voices of those most affected by change.

User needs versus business needs

Ensuring all outputs and outcomes of our work are truly user centred represents a real challenge, as many organisations still separate out business processes, strategy and operations from digital delivery. By only focusing on business requirements, we risk shaping our solutions in ways that could be hard for people to access or that don't enable them to achieve their goals. Likewise, by focusing only on user needs we can fail to answer crucial questions of scale, and the cost of running and maintaining services and technology solutions.

Approached successfully, balancing both sets of needs means building services in ways that are modern and efficient, as well as delivering the best possible outcomes for people. The key is learning to hold problems to solve in both hands. In one hand, we can hold on to user needs – the goals people have, and the types of outcomes we are working towards. While in the other hand we hold on to our business goals, motivations, constraints, and the reasoning behind the work. A design mindset is our ability to continuously put people at the centre of both of these perspectives. Even when working with business goals and constraints, we can be intentional about making links back to how each internal decision will affect external experiences and outcomes.

Working with conflict and tensions

The pull between seemingly opposing forces such as business and user needs can enable new ideas and solutions to emerge, if we are willing to try out new approaches.

When there are tensions and disagreements inside our organisations between operational, policy, and delivery teams, it's an opportunity to work together to create something far better than we previously thought possible. As British journalist Ian Leslie explains in his book, *Conflicted*: "[disagreement is] an act of creativity in itself. A purposeful disagreement can take two plus two and make five. What defines a pointless disagreement? I think it's a disagreement that isn't interested in creating something new . . . When two opposing ideas clash, the optimal solution is to create a third".[56]

Even when there are differences, applying a design mindset means always being willing to work together towards creating something new. Some of the most powerful working sessions arise from putting people from different functions together in a room, including those with different perspectives and even conflicting priorities. When we focus on creating shared understanding, and take responsibility for owning problems together, collaboration becomes a multiplier. Bringing the right people together in the same room – even if that room now needs to be a virtual space – gives us the opportunity to create something better.[57]

Simplicity with complexity

Applying a design mindset is crucial to helping people work together in complex systems, supporting how they increase the reach and impact of their work and improve outcomes.

For something to be complex really just means that it consists of many different and connected component parts and relationships. When designing and delivering public services, all of the systems we work within – including technology, policy, and operations – are inherently complex. Although organisations might want to improve outcomes for users, change can be deemed too hard to even attempt.

However, with a design mindset, simplicity and complexity are not necessarily opposites. We can have complexity in the work, but use simplicity in our approaches to delivering the work.[58]

This means that simplicity is a multiplier – used effectively, it helps teams make faster progress and work in a focused way. It is also why design specialists are an important part of multidisciplinary teams. When designers create simple visual artefacts, such as maps, it gives us the ability to zoom in and out on specific parts of systems, operating processes and user journeys. This brings new perspectives and helps teams navigate their way through work effectively.

Simplicity can also be starting with one thing, or identifying and testing a key assumption, and then being willing to go back and conduct research where there are gaps in knowledge or understanding. Most of all, it's our ability to break down and understand the component parts of something more complex – this is also known as working from first principles and is something we will return to in chapter 6.

All of this requires a design mindset that is willing to question the approach being taken, ensuring that teams remain focused on shaping and delivering the best possible outcomes.

Doing the hard work to make things simple

Simplicity is not just about how we approach our work. It should also be reflected in the end products and the quality of solutions that we are able to deliver.

This is where good design can actually mean as little design as possible, or as the German industrial designer Dieter Rams sets out: "less, but better."[59] Applying this to the public sector's work, we need teams to create solutions that are simple to understand and use. This is reflected in one of the ten UK Government Design Principles: "Do the hard work to make it simple".[60] It means removing processes, content, and user interactions that are confusing or unnecessary, and designing more intuitive, joined up experiences. Importantly, it also means dealing with legacy technology, operational, and policy considerations.

Addressing these types of constraints often involves complex work with multiple dependencies, but with the right mindset it is possible. For example, when the Department for Work and Pensions (DWP) delivered their first live digital exemplar on GOV.UK, the team managed to remove 170 questions from the existing application process for Carer's Allowance – 49% of the questions.[61] Not only did this mean designing and testing content in new ways, it involved working closely with policy teams to challenge requirements around data capture and the amount of personal information needed from service users. This contributed significantly to the creation of a more efficient, faster and simpler service.

Asking design questions

To take a design mindset and turn this into something more practical we need teams and individuals to ask design questions.[62] This is a way of maintaining focus, creating shared understanding, and directing how decisions are made.

As a starting point, a basic framework for any digital transformation initiative is for teams to answer the following questions:

- **Why are we doing this work?**
  Understanding the reasoning and motivation behind any work that is being proposed, or has been started.

- **Who are our users?**
  Being able to describe who we think will need to use a service or solution.

- **What outcome will users get from this service?**
  Being able to describe why we think people will use a service or solution.

- **What outcome are we looking for?**
  Explaining the problem from the perspective of our organisation, and any operational constraints and problems to solve internally.

- **What are our key metrics?**
  Explaining how we intend to measure progress against these outcomes as we deliver the work.

You will find variations on these questions in lots of different approaches to design thinking, but they are all based around the same broad principles. To start with, it's important to take an honest look at the motivations behind any new policy, service or programme of work. We need to begin by understanding why we have been asked to design or build something in the first place. It might be something as simple as a senior leader deciding that an initiative is a good idea, or it might be that we are responding to a significant political announcement or policy decision.

Understanding why work has been commissioned means we can start to acknowledge obvious constraints such as policy decisions, or the overall intended scope of the work. As we introduced in chapter 3, there is also a need for organisations to give teams more autonomy and accountability for service outcomes in the policy areas they work with. This means that digital delivery teams must be empowered to push back and influence these types of commissioning decisions, challenging the reasoning behind work, and how starting requirements are agreed.

Once we have understood the motivation behind the work it makes it possible to dig deeper. We need to understand who users really are, what problem we are trying to solve, and how this aligns with any business needs or objectives. This includes how we define purpose and vision and use this to guide decision making. And finally, we need to know how to measure success. How we will determine when we have delivered the right outcomes?

All of this is what is known as framing the problem.[63] If these questions seem simple, it's because they are. But it's surprising how often teams do not have a shared understanding of the answers. Another risk is that these questions are asked once at the initiation of new work, and then not revisited in the lifetime of delivery. Instead, with a design mindset we revisit these types of questions consistently throughout our work, keeping activities aligned to meeting the right needs and goals.

Challenging assumptions

Our ability to challenge assumptions at key points of a project is always vital to the success and eventual impact of work. As an example of where this could have been done better we can look at HS2, the high speed railway project linking London to towns and cities in the Midlands and the North of England. The project has encountered a number of problems throughout its lifetime, running further and further over budget with costs rising by billions of pounds.

One of the most controversial parts of HS2 is the cost-benefit analysis that was used to justify the original project. As reported in 2019, when making the original business case, planners assumed that no passengers would work while on a train. This made the time savings on the new line look more valuable than they really were.[64]

As this shows, it's important to understand and question the types of underlying assumptions that shape decisions, especially when these decisions lead to significant amounts of public money being invested. In this case research and data about existing rail passengers could have been considered much earlier as part of initial consultations and planning processes. This might have then shaped a different focus in the business case set out to key decision makers. For example, it could have been that upgrading wifi, or increasing the frequency of trains on existing lines would have delivered as much, or even more value, at less cost and with less disruption than HS2.

The most useful design questions can simply revert back to someone being willing to ask "why is this work a priority?" or, "how do we know we are focusing on the right problem to solve?" This is as applicable for major policy and national infrastructure investments, as it is for investment in services and organisation change.

To use a technology example, one aspect highlighted in the government's first attempts to build a NHS Covid-19 contact tracing app is that no one associated with the project could explain what the app would actually be used for. While there was clearly an assumption that an app was needed, the move to develop something at the start of the pandemic reportedly happened without any clear idea of what this app was trying to do. This contributed to time being wasted and technology decisions that later had to be abandoned as the government was forced to change its approach.[65]

When applying a design mindset, and as highlighted by this example, it can be most useful to simply imagine that any starting requirements are wrong. Most importantly, teams must always be prepared to constructively question what they're asked to deliver, and the policy decisions they are working with.

As Anthony King and Ivor Crewe explain in their book *The Blunders of Our Governments,* there is a need to continually challenge assumptions. They suggest that: "there always needs to be 'grit in the oyster', at least one person present in all discussions with the task of arguing the case on the other side. This means finding potential defects in what otherwise seems an unassailable proposition."[66] Without this type of challenge, projects risk suffering from "group-think", where teams and decision makers are totally focused on doing something, but forget to ask themselves whether it's the right thing to do.

Extending design questioning

If we are serious about extending the reach and impact of digital transformation we also have to question our choices much more carefully, considering the effects of all decisions we make on the places and communities we are working with.[67]

Teams should be actively considering who might be excluded as a result of design or policy choices, understanding how solutions might fail to reach people with specific needs, and then focusing time and effort on how to address this. This also includes what happens when solutions themselves fail, or don't work as intended – especially when they are exposed to a wider range of individual circumstances and complex needs.

By committing to asking design questions about a broader range of potential scenarios, we can make more informed decisions. How we answer questions may also highlight the need for more detailed research with excluded groups, and people with specific needs. If we are serious about putting other people's experiences and perspectives at the centre of how public services are delivered, then we need to become better at listening and learning. We can then create solutions that are more adaptable to future scenarios, designing in a much more considered way for when things inevitably change or turn out differently from how we expect them to.

New ways of managing risk and uncertainty

A particular change in mindset needed for digital transformation is in how organisations and teams work with risk and uncertainty. Whereas traditionally, risk management in technology delivery has relied on careful planning, with detailed requirement gathering processes, a design mindset helps us work in new ways, deal with ambiguity, and design for unknown situations – managing uncertainty by learning through doing.

This is a key component of a design mindset: a bias towards action. It is the belief that we can always achieve more by taking a decisive step forward, creating something to test, and then learning from what happens. Most importantly, it's always about doing something rather than trying to mitigate risk or unknowns through more planning and theorising. A lesson from the last decade of digital transformation is that the energy we spend talking about something is the same energy and focus we should be spending doing something.

When speed trumps perfection

Starting is often the hardest part of change, and there will always be a tension between needing to take a first step, and knowing which step to take. But we believe doing something faster is often far more effective than not acting at all.

We have seen this tension demonstrated in the different types of responses around the world to the pandemic. Speaking at a virtual press conference on March 13th 2020 – two weeks before the UK went into full lockdown, Dr Michael J Ryan, an Executive Director at the World Health Organisation (WHO) said this: "If you need to be right before you move, you will never win. Perfection is the enemy of the good when it comes to emergency management. Speed trumps perfection. And the problem in society we have at the moment, is that everyone is afraid of making a mistake, everyone is afraid of the consequence of error. But the greatest error is not to move. The greatest error is to be paralysed by the fear of failure. That's the single biggest lesson I've learnt."[68]

Dr Ryan has been at the forefront of managing acute risks to global health for nearly 25 years, and the mindset of a bias towards action he describes here is something we should learn from in how we respond to change in the future.

Ambiguity and design

The concept of learning by doing also brings into question how teams deal with ambiguity, or not knowing. Ambiguity points us to the uncomfortable gap between "what is" and "what could be".

The future we are working towards is full of unknowns. As former US Defense Secretary Donald Rumsfeld famously stated in 2002: "There are things we know we know. We also know there are known unknowns; that is to say we know there are some things we do not know. But there are also unknown unknowns – the ones we don't know we don't know."[69]

There will always be many directions and possibilities open to us in any decision we need to make – from policy, to operations and service design. But teams have to be capable of making progress in changing situations and without always knowing what will happen next.[70] This is where a design mindset is beneficial. Approaches to how we work with ambiguity and unknowns can then mean:

- not needing to have all the answers before we start – responding to research and insights while accepting that there are still unknown unknowns that will affect our decisions
- taking more intuitive leaps – using divergent thinking to explore new ideas and different ways of solving problems or designing experiences
- holding strong opinions and being willing to explore opposing ideas
- developing bold ideas that are different to existing models of the world – starting to understand the gaps between future models we are creating, and what exists now
- being confident enough to simplify ideas within complex systems – asking questions like: how would we design this if we started again today?

Test and learn approaches

The attitude we have towards failure, and the way we manage risk and uncertainty is also key if we are going to see more radical change to how teams meet changing needs and future challenges. If we look back on over a decade of digital transformation, there is much to learn from the success of agile delivery, including how teams gather evidence and build certainty that their work is delivering the right solutions in the right ways. This has demonstrated that the most effective way to approach change is to use a test and learn approach. By limiting the size of each change we make and seeing what happens, we are able to respond to unknowns, changing direction where and when necessary.

We can see this shift in mindset increasingly influencing how government departments deliver major programmes of work. Janet Hughes is currently a transformation leader at the Department for Environment, Food & Rural Affairs (Defra). Representing the Future Farming programme at a committee in summer 2021, Janet described how Defra are managing the risk and uncertainty following previous failures of digital transformation in the Department: "I am confident, and the reason . . . is that we're not taking a big bang approach to implementing these changes . . . [instead we're taking] an incremental test and learn approach, so we introduce a change, we see how it goes, we learn from that and we introduce the next stage."[71]

This approach enables organisations to treat every change they make as a series of controlled experiments. These are designed to provide the most efficient possible way to test new ideas, or to gradually increase the scale and complexity of different solutions. This way, teams get to evaluate and respond to what really happens, taking incremental steps to manage risk in delivery. This is also where design specialists are needed to support experiments, creating the right artefacts or models to test, and working closely with user researchers and data analysts to ensure that changes are evaluated in the right ways, and that progress is measurable.

We can also extend this beyond testing and evaluating digital solutions. Through processes of prototyping and piloting teams can test new approaches to everything from team structures and ways of working to models for in person support. Using test and learn approaches across business functions is the best way of ensuring that any new uses of technology are evaluated in the context of real operational delivery.

Hypothesis based design

Applying a design mindset means ensuring that there are processes in place to incorporate test and learn approaches as part of delivery. This way of working is often described as hypothesis based design. For this to be successful, teams have to be clear about the reasoning behind each design decision they intend to take, and agree what they expect to happen when a change is delivered. The key process is then how they consistently capture and prioritise hypotheses to test, revisiting these regularly as part of each delivery cycle. Working in this way, it's possible to think of every decision taken in agile delivery as being hypothesis based.[72]

For teams to be accountable for their design decisions, it's important for every change to a product or service to be tracked and measured. This then helps teams to understand if they are solving problems and making progress towards overall goals in the right ways.

Collective small actions

The final question to return to is how we continue to shape behaviours and mindsets in the places we work and with the people around us, in order to bring about the outcomes we want to achieve.

We can all be deliberate with every small action we take every day, aligning our behaviours to shared values and goals.[73] Mindset and behaviour change is often slow and gradual, but we all have a circle of influence within our immediate work. The important thing to remember is that small actions demonstrated consistently by individuals start to influence what happens collectively.

If there is one principle that we can all adopt, it's "keep going". This simply means turning up each day with the determination to consistently apply the same set of behaviours and attitudes – no matter how radical this thinking, and type of questioning, might seem at the time. We can all begin to act like multipliers, knowing that others are working with us, and that the only way to move something the size of an organisation is to gradually build momentum, coordinating how we work together.

We can change that

With a design mindset the possibilities for digital transformation are endless.

In this chapter we have explored how we can think and act in new ways. We have looked at the importance of using simplicity in our work, our ability to challenge assumptions, and the need to ask better design questions. We have also seen that a change of mindset requires a bias towards action. This is how we can manage uncertainty and risk as we learn by doing, helping our organisations and teams to become more comfortable with ambiguity.

With a design mindset we can question what is possible. This is how our teams will ultimately be able to meet changing expectations for future services, while also creating better outcomes for individuals and society.

In the next chapter we will look at how the relationship the public sector has with technology needs to change, enabling us to think and work in new ways.

Multiplied Thinking: Key takeaways from chapter 4

- **Adopt a design mindset.** Recognise the importance of being able to think and act differently, ensuring that teams are capable of responding to future challenges.

- **Make all work user centred.** Place people and their needs at the centre of all delivery and business activities. Create opportunities for everyone to observe, and to work more closely with service users and real life situations.

- **Use simplicity.** Work towards simple, intuitive solutions, while dealing with constraints like policy. Use simple models and visual design approaches as an approach to working with complex systems.

- **Ask design questions.** Be prepared to challenge underlying assumptions, and frame problems clearly. This provides focus, and creates shared understanding to support improved outcomes through better design decisions.

- **Think differently about risk and uncertainty.** Use incremental test and learn approaches, with hypothesis based design to manage unknowns when delivering digital transformation.

- **Start with collective small actions.** Ask teams and individuals to be deliberate with every action they take each day, aligning behaviours to shared values and goals.

5 Technology as an enabler of change

"People are talking to their governments on 21st century technology . . . governments listen to them on 20th century technology and provide 19th century responses"

– Madeleine Albright[74]

To achieve greater impact, every organisation delivering public services needs to be good at information technology (IT). This includes any use of computers, networks, devices, infrastructure and processes to create, store, and share electronic data. To deliver improved services, making better use of modern, reliable technologies has to be at the heart of our thinking.

It's important to start by saying that we already have access to many of the tools, solutions and approaches we need. But the relationship our organisations have with technology can be described as complicated and costly. Its introduction to the public sector over previous decades hasn't always led to the type of transformation that many of us would hope for, with many public services under performing despite technology investment, and sometimes even because of it.

How we successfully respond to future challenges will depend on how we select technology, how we manage it, and how we use it. Each of these considerations is essential if we're to deliver the changes our front line services need. To do this we will need new types of solutions to unlock the full potential and reach of services through digital transformation.

Digital beyond the IT department

The IT department was first introduced into most businesses sometime in the 1980s. Its functions involved installing and maintaining computer networks, supplying and managing software for staff, and providing supporting infrastructure to keep things running smoothly. In many businesses IT has grown from small teams into what is often one of the largest and most powerful departments (at least in terms of budget).

The introduction of digital ways of working into organisations has challenged the idea that technology should be the responsibility of one team or department. Digital has also reset expectations around how technology should be used. This is no longer just about the tools we need to run a business – technology is increasingly the primary way that people access services. It's how they choose to communicate with our organisations, and it's now at the core of how internet era businesses work.

That said, there are many institutions that still retain the business models of the last century, including many parts of the public sector where it's still all too common to find IT functioning more as a separate department and internal service provider. This means that IT departments still see the rest of the organisations they are part of as their customers, with a supplier-buyer relationship, albeit one without any competition or choice.

While many IT departments have been responsible for providing technology capabilities, few have historically been capable of building software. As a consequence most solutions or services have to be bought in and managed through external suppliers. The immediate risk is that budget holders and those managing specifications are not close enough to the needs of staff or the citizens solutions are intended for.

This way of working continues to lead to a lack of creativity in how organisations build, buy and use technology. It emphasises delivering to a plan — even when that plan is wrong. It lacks the flexibility to move away from upfront requirements and respond to changing needs and situations.

It is also important to reflect that the investment in digital over the past decade hasn't solved this problem. If anything, it has simply highlighted, and even amplified, some of the same issues caused by traditional IT approaches. This is because – in the same way as the IT departments of the past were siloed – many digital programmes also function separately from the wider organisations they are part of. Where IT wasn't deemed able to meet their needs, organisations have set up digital teams and programmes hoping for a fresh, more responsive approach to technology delivery. But it has become increasingly clear that setting up digital teams alongside IT doesn't work, as it only leads to tension and conflict.

Reshaping our relationship with technology

Internet enabled devices and connected technologies are now so intertwined with our everyday lives that the lines are blurred between our digital and real life experiences.

In the same way, we can no longer think about technology as a separate layer of our work. Whether it's a department, or a set of capabilities and solutions to be managed, technology has to be at the heart of our approach. In practical terms, this means anyone working with technology in our public institutions should see the rest of their organisation as their colleagues, not their customers. It also has implications for an age old debate in the technology world, that of build versus buy.

The cost of building software used to be so high that it mostly made sense to buy solutions. But factor in the customisation and upgrades required for enterprise technology, along with licence costs and expensive technical support, and this choice isn't as straightforward as it seems. It's not all about financial costs either. An off the shelf solution might never work in a way that suits an organisation, forcing staff to adapt to the needs of the technology, rather than the other way round. These are the life long inefficiencies of bought solutions. When systems are not designed to meet user needs, manual workarounds such as increased data entry create frustration and burden staff with technical stress.

Today, modern organisations really should have the ability to build and deploy their own digital solutions, and the changing technology landscape means that it's now much easier to build, test and deliver software yourself at pace. New approaches to technology increasingly abstract away a lot of the technical infrastructure or "plumbing" needed to build solutions, so options no longer have to be reduced to the costs of comparing build or buy. Solutions can instead be conceived and designed with the input of people who will ultimately have to use them, and built by teams with a shared interest in making them work well.

Right now, the money still being spent on enterprise technology is investment that could be made in building the next generation of software and services for the public sector. More organisations working in this way, with the right approaches to shared solutions will benefit everyone.

For a preview of this new reality, we can look to the private sector. Most internet era startups don't have separate IT departments. In these organisations, the lines between who supplies technology, who works with it and who delivers technology solutions are blurred so much, they no longer exist. These are organisations that reflect the world they're part of. A world where everything – from the global economy, to the services and systems we interact with everyday – runs on software and technology. You simply can't be a modern service organisation without technology as part of your DNA.

A mindset shift for managers and leaders

What we are describing also requires a change at the management and leadership levels of our organisations. The people leading our organisations and teams don't necessarily need to be hands on with technology – these are different skill sets from overseeing complex organisations and programmes of work. But just as any "us and them" mentality between teams and IT departments needs to be torn down, so too must the wall between those who sign off on technology investment and the people who deliver it.

This calls for bold leadership, and a break away from traditional executive boards which don't have a place for technology. It means the introduction of Chief Digital and Information Officers (CDIOs) who bring modern technology thinking that is then truly represented in decision making, and considered as a critical part of an organisation's long term strategic goals.

The importance of this can't be underestimated. Many of today's leaders have not grown up with technology and internet era services in the same way that our future leaders will have. But they must still be able to understand technology, including its opportunities and constraints. Only by having a grasp of what technology can and can't do, and how opportunities are changing, can they steer their organisations and teams effectively, both now and in the future.

Technology enabled organisations

For technology to be a multiplier the approach that modern public institutions need is one of complete integration, with technical and digital capabilities flowing through every part of the organisation.

Technology can also support and enable new business models and innovation, as well as a focus on user outcomes. With technology thinking and skills, autonomous teams are empowered to explore new opportunities during the design and implementation of services. This means they should always have the freedom to choose the appropriate technologies they need to try new things.

How we build

When resetting the relationship our organisations have with technology, flexibility is key.

This is particularly important in the public sector, as the responsibilities attached to public institutions are much more complex than most commercial enterprises. In the private sector, businesses can reduce complexity by optimising their supply chains and focusing on creating value for a specific target market. But the public sector has to meet multiple, changing sets of needs for all of society. The goal is to provide the tools, support, or services needed to deliver the best possible outcomes and support for staff and citizens, so it's unlikely that any single technology or all in one solution will be the answer.

A key principle of taking a more flexible approach is small and connected solutions. This kind of technology can be described as loosely-coupled, since the structure of services – known as their architecture – breaks down applications into component functions which are all built and managed separately.

In loosely-coupled architectures, such as microservices, individual parts of a service communicate with each other in highly defined ways, through well managed Application Programming Interfaces (APIs). They are therefore much more flexible, resilient, and easier to maintain. This is in direct contrast to solutions that are built as one large, complex service, where a single point of failure can bring down the entire application, as each process relies directly on another.

Working with the right technology foundations is a multiplier, as we can deliver more effective and more efficient solutions through loosely-coupled approaches. When software capabilities are separate, but linked functions, they can be added to or removed seamlessly as services scale and adapt to changing business needs over time. Everything is customised, built, and integrated to the exact needs of the organisation and the services it delivers. This flexibility is also how we can best meet user needs.

Modern technology approaches also remove the complexity of having to host and maintain many elements of critical IT infrastructure. By outsourcing these capabilities to commercial cloud providers such as AWS, Microsoft, or Google through services including Serverless computing, Platform as a Service (PaaS), and Software as a Service (SaaS), technical delivery teams can focus on creating applications, rather than managing the supporting technology.

The legacy of open source thinking

When working with a loosely-coupled approach, a key principle of modern technology delivery is to only solve the problems we need to solve. Whatever our choices, and the combination of choices we make, it simply doesn't make sense to custom build solutions that already exist. The important thing is that we always look sideways first – "not invented here" does not mean "not useful here".'[75]

To promote the sharing and repurposing of solutions, the GOV.UK and NHS service standards, as well as the Local Digital Declaration encourage delivery teams to make source code open. Specifically this means they must "make all new source code open and reusable, and publish it under appropriate licences".[76] As the GOV.UK Service Manual sets out: "when you create new source code, you must make it open so that other developers (including those outside government) can: benefit from your work and build on it; learn from your experiences; [and] find uses for your code which you had not found."[77] This has been a success story of many digital transformation projects to date, with the open sourcing of code in repositories such as GitHub leading to great examples of code being shared across organisations, saving time and effort. It has also been seen during the Covid-19 pandemic with teams able to build quickly on the work of others when creating new services.

As part of their Covid-19 response, for example, Essex County Council built a directory of services to help support children and families. A digital solution was created, building on open source code from directories already developed by teams in Camden and Buckinghamshire. As the Essex team explained when they first launched the service: "We know these organisations and we trust them . . . They had done the hard work and were happy to share it. It made sense to use this as the foundation for what we were building."[78]

Although we recognise the need to share code and have built this into our own practices, it's important to understand that a commitment to open source doesn't solve problems on its own. There is still considerable effort required to customise and adapt code that has been shared elsewhere – with teams often having to reshape whole digital solutions in order to make them useful in new contexts.

Low code and no-code solutions

The improvement and increase of solutions in the low code and no-code software space also offers interesting possibilities for organisations looking to build their own products and services. We have seen a marked increase in organisations taking this approach to creating digital solutions.

Low code and no-code is software that reduces, or completely removes the need to code altogether when building digital solutions. Low and no-code tools typically offer drag and drop functionalities, meaning that they're simple to use, but aren't always suitable for building highly customised or complex applications (although this is changing as the tools evolve). At a basic level, they should enable teams to create web forms and pages quickly, and when done right, build digital solutions that are accessible and that fully meet Web Content Accessibility Guidelines (WCAG). These types of solutions are a growing trend, especially as technical skills and experience remain difficult for parts of the public sector to access. That said, even when businesses do have available software engineering expertise, they still might choose no-code tools to build simple applications, as their developers' time could be better spent elsewhere.[79]

These opportunities come with a word of caution. With the growing range of vendor software solutions now available in this space there is also a growing range of costs and subscription models. This might leave organisations with additional overheads due to vendor lock in and regular upgrades to manage. It's also true that not all low code and no-code software creates fully accessible solutions that follow best practice. While vendor solutions may provide a short cut, if you look underneath the surface, you may still find inferior quality code that doesn't meet the high standards set by in house development teams building custom solutions. This can lead to both poor application performance and accessibility issues.

Overall, these options can be useful, but often only in limited ways. If you have many existing or simple transactions to move online then a low code or no-code solution makes sense – this is the sort of thing a local council might need to do cheaply and quickly if they still rely on paper processes. But this limits organisations to digitisation, and there needs to come a point where the continued existence of these types of digital transactions is called into question. When services are completely redesigned and rebuilt, it's unlikely that low and no-code software tools will be flexible enough or capable of supporting this type of change.

The important thing is to carefully evaluate any tools your organisation invests in. In the end, the opportunity is to support faster and more automated delivery while still carefully managing costs. As an example of one such success story, the Ministry of Justice Form Builder (which is also open sourced), now provides the department with a low code platform with less need for specialist development resources. This has already been used to create more than a dozen digital transactions for the department on GOV.UK, showing what is possible without third party vendor solutions and cost overheads.[80]

Platform thinking

Perhaps more important than open source code is the introduction of digital platforms as a widely adopted tool in public service delivery.

In chapter 1 we considered the history of the Government Digital Service (GDS), including their Government as a Platform (GaaP) strategy. Launched in 2015 as the next step for digital government, this was a plan to put a common core infrastructure of shared digital systems, technology and processes in place for teams across government. As GDS described, the vision for GaaP was to enable more teams to build brilliant, user centred government services.[81]

In the years since its launch, GaaP has built initiatives such as GOV.UK Notify and Pay. These have given the public sector new tools to deliver services using common solutions. Just as importantly, both the GDS and NHS Design System, and front end toolkits, are platforms that have provided teams with reusable code, and tried and tested design patterns, enabling faster and more efficient ways of building services. As the NHS Service Manual explains, these support the build of consistent, accessible user interfaces, enabling different teams to learn from the research and the experience of others.[82]

Tim Paul, Head of Interaction Design at GDS, shared in 2020 that the GOV.UK Design System had 1500 open source repositories on GitHub, representing the work of about 300 distinct UK government services. This created an estimated saving for the government of over £17 million a year. Economists in GDS came up with this figure based on how many teams use the Design System; how often people in those teams use the tools; how much more productive teams are using the tools; and what people would do if the tools didn't exist – also taking into account average salaries and churn rates of specialists working in government, with the final figure representing the additional cost to the government of delivering services of a similar quality without a Design System.[83]

To give an idea of the further savings made through platform thinking, GOV.UK Notify is by far the best example we have so far: this simple platform allows public sector bodies and local authorities to send people important messages. These range from council tax reminders to details of doctors appointments. In 2019 Notify was forecast to save taxpayers an average of £35 million a year over the next 5 years.[84] In May 2020, Pete Herlihy, former Lead Product Manager for Notify shared that the platform had just sent its 1 billionth message, less than four years after going live. More recently, in March 2021 alone Notify sent 205 million notifications – the busiest month ever for the platform – with many of these messages being Covid-19 test results and vaccination bookings, and with predicted total savings set to dwarf the original 2019 forecast.[85]

As with all these examples, platform approaches succeed when they're built using agile delivery, relying on user research to test and iterate a service with teams across the public sector. Most importantly, this means taking the time to understand different types of user needs and use cases.

The future of Government as a Platform

To reflect further on Government as a Platform. Services like GOV.UK Notify have already created enormous value and flexibility for teams across the public sector. But what if we were to extend this thinking?

In local government for example, there is enormous potential for shared platforms and systems. We said earlier that the investments needed to license and support enterprise technology solutions could be better used to build the next generation of products and services. This could represent a new generation of shared platforms that support social care, housing, and education. The same is true in the wider health system, where there are hundreds of hospital trusts across the UK needing solutions to support the digital transformation of front line services.

The challenge is how we collectively invest more in common platforms, both through how they're developed and then how they are maintained. These don't only have to come from central organisations like GDS and NHS Digital. Greater numbers of technology solutions built and configured by local teams could also be turned into platforms for reuse, creating shared solutions for live services across the sector. This is a logical progression from open sourcing and is about encouraging organisations to work more closely together.

Local government is already leading some of the most promising work in this area. The Local Digital Declaration – designed to support a new generation of local public services – was first launched in 2018, with many councils signing up to the commitments it sets out. As the declaration describes, technology should be an enabler rather than a barrier to service improvements in local government. It also clearly states an ambition around platform solutions, which it describes as fixing the plumbing. This is the intention to break away from dependencies on inflexible and expensive technology that doesn't join up effectively, instead "insisting on modular building blocks for the IT we rely on, and open standards to give a common structure to the data we create."[86] As we have already seen with GaaP, this idea of modular building blocks will also be increasingly important in future services at a local level.

The Local Digital Fund,[87] which aims to help local authorities implement the Local Digital Declaration, has since financed a number of projects, including the development of shared solutions that are then co-owned by different councils. These range from a "tell us once" service – a discovery exploring the best way of allowing people moving into an area to contact the council just once to set up all their services

– to a back office planning system, with five council partners working together on this project, and sharing all the details in the open.[88]

As long as different organisations need a number of common capabilities or services then there is an opportunity for more shared solutions such as these. With more organisations working together to build the next generation of shared platforms, there will simply be no excuse for more costly and inefficient alternatives. However, it's important to note that these services must be managed in the right way. APIs, for example, require maintenance to keep them up to date with the systems they provide access to, and with any changes to data formats or security requirements. If this work is not carried out, or not completed carefully enough, technology services will go down.

Platform business models for the public sector

In the private sector, modern businesses are already making the most of loosely-coupled solutions and integration with SaaS functionality. But there is also a different type of platform thinking that has emerged over the past decade. This is demonstrated in the number of successful startups that have created entirely new business models by becoming technology platforms themselves.

Platform business models invert traditional business models by unlocking spare capacity. Generally, this means harnessing contributions from a community outside of an organisation. Any platform business must therefore shift its focus from internal to external activities to tap into new possibilities and potential. This is at the heart of internet enabled businesses like Airbnb and Uber.

With Airbnb, the spare capacity is people's private property which they're able to rent out via a digital platform, connecting them directly to the demand created by people looking for places to stay. This business model doesn't require them to own any hotels. They simply run the platform which connects visitors to a host – anyone with a spare room or accommodation. With Uber the same business model applies. The platform connects people needing a lift with drivers, and takes care of bookings and payments. The business model doesn't require Uber to own a taxi fleet, or even to treat their drivers as employees (although the law around this is changing, and there are ethical questions here too).[89]

These platform models dramatically lowers transaction costs on both sides. Platforms provide those offering services with a pool of potential customers, remove the hassle of managing bookings and payments, and reduce risk – like that of renting your home or car to a stranger.[90] Those looking for services get similar benefits – with a wide range of options to choose from, and a level of security from transacting via the platform instead of directly with the vendor. To make this work platform businesses need to provide assurances so that people will trust their service. Airbnb does this by providing hosts with financial insurance. This guarantees people renting out their homes compensation if anything goes wrong and their property is damaged, as well as reimbursing guests if the accommodation is not as advertised.

In spite of its success in the private sector, the use of platforms to disrupt existing business models is largely untapped in the public sector. Yet this is an opportunity to explore how our public institutions manage capacity around service demand to meet needs and expectations. It is their ability to deliver more impact through new business models and create greater benefits for people. In the public sector, platform thinking might ask: how could a council operate as a platform to improve mental health outcomes? And how could they make better use of links into their local community, as well as into third sector and voluntary organisations to do this?

Again, it's important to recognise that front line services already play a vital role in connecting and referring people to places where they can get the most relevant support. But what if technology played a more significant part in this, reducing costs for local authorities and extending the reach and relevance of referrals?

Platform examples in public services

There are already some experiments that we can point to in this space. Working with local authorities in Essex and Suffolk, we have helped to design platform models for government subsidised bus services. This included the piloting of on demand bus routes in rural areas that were designed to unlock spare capacity from local private taxi firms.

Used in the right way, platform models like this create the opportunity to build and expand services around existing social connections. In chapter 3, we highlighted Parkinson's Connect, the new support model being offered by Parkinson's UK. As organisations look to use technology to transform how they work, platforms like this are an opportunity to extend the reach of the support they offer. With the right design, concepts like peer to peer support, and increasing community connections, can be part of how services adapt to changing needs. This is platform thinking that enables us to think more about personalised and targeted services, all facilitated by technology.

As with our responsive transport example, this type of platform thinking has mostly been in the stages of early experimentation in the public sector. But there are exceptions. Casserole Club is a meal sharing service which was first founded in 2011. The concept was designed to connect people who like to cook with their older neighbours who aren't always able to cook for themselves. It's a simple platform that, through providing people with a way to share home cooked meals, eventually reached over 7,000 people in England and Australia. Meal Makers (a subsidiary of the award winning Scottish charity Food Train), adapted and launched the Casserole Club model in Scotland. Launched in Dundee in 2011, they've grown to a network across 10 local authorities that has connected over 6000 chefs, with over 1000 people who have received home cooked meals. Meal Makers have also adapted to continue connecting people with meals during the Covid-19 pandemic, with appropriate Covid-19 measures and support in place.[91]

This example in particular is technology creating direct ways to extend support, with services being sustained in communities, and in large part by volunteers. Running the platform can be done at minimal cost as the technology is relatively cheap, but the platform does enough to connect supply to demand. Most of all it builds relationships, with neighbours often meeting each other for the first time when they join these initiatives. This creates new community connections that can lead to long term friendships as well as stronger, more self sustaining community networks.

Platform thinking is a multiplier. This requires organisations to organise in ways that will unlock their strongest assets, the systems and places they work within, and the relationships they have that connect all of these things together. The biggest question then becomes: how can we change the way we deliver services, including the way we work with external communities and partners, to increase our impact?

Once we're willing to explore these new models, one further question arises. This is to what extent this type of change is even possible with the existing political and organisational leadership we have in place. The people that have seen the opportunities of technology platforms as business models aren't the same people traditionally leading large corporations in the private sector, never mind the public sector. But maybe this is also an opportunity for the public sector to lead by example. To move and innovate first, so that platform business models are no longer seen as the exclusive domain of technology startups.

Digital innovation enabled by existing technologies

It's easy to fall into the trap of thinking we need new types of innovation through technology to solve our most difficult or pressing problems. The pandemic has shown us otherwise. Most of the fast, effective responses from the public sector have been made possible by existing technology. In the majority of cases, it was our mindset and our relationship to technology that needed to change.

There's a more useful definition of what innovation means here. It doesn't have to be about making something new, it can be about resetting the existing order of things.[92]

Enabling people to make better uses of the tools and solutions that are already available to them is especially important when time and resources are limited. During the pandemic, for example, this was seen in community action coordinated through WhatsApp groups and Facebook. In the first lockdown of 2020, neighbours were able to connect with each other, organising supplies like food and medication. Even basic technologies like SMS text messages were enough to help groups coordinate, and to stay connected as society changed overnight.

This type of organising is not new, and we have already seen local services for strengthening community connections designed around existing platforms. As an example, Tower Hamlets Council first set about tackling the serious problem of loneliness in their local area in 2017 by focusing on how sites like Facebook could be used to connect people in the community. They have continued investing significantly into a project that now connects over 50s with activities, local services and each other. One particular initiative has involved matching care home residents with volunteers based on common interests, such as doing crosswords, in a bid to boost social interaction.[93]

We are still at the beginning of exploring the potential uses of technology to create new types of services and operational models in the public sector. But more impact is possible as long as we're ready to question how we organise, connect with and reach people in society. This type of work will require a willingness for more rapid experimentation, and an openness to use the technology we already have in new ways.

Putting technology to work on harder problems

When presented with the challenges and opportunities of digital trans-formation, we have a tendency to prioritise easier problems. As Tom Goodwin, author of *Digital Darwinism* sets out, when we embark on a digital transformation journey, we rightly start out with projects that are easy and make a big difference. But then we also get stuck in making easy, yet pointless, additions – rather than tackling more systemic and harder challenges.

We know this is true of the public sector because it's the case in every sector. To apply Tom's thinking again, it explains why high street banks offer user friendly smartphone apps while their accounting sys-tems are still running on code developed decades ago. Or why you can order food for your flight on an iPad in the airport lounge, yet if you'd wanted to change your flight the day before, you'd have been on hold to an operator for 25 minutes. Every time, the superficial trumps the truly transformative when it comes to business models and joined up services. Changing an organisation's relationship with technology is therefore the first step to revisiting its priorities as we look to the future of digital transformation.

In chapter 1 we talked about the limits of public sector digital transformation programmes over the previous decade. How digitisation has allowed us to do many of the same things, differently – moving analogue processes and services online. But the focus now has to be dig-italisation: transforming services and core business models. This means business activities and new ways of working enabled by technology.

In the same way that businesses can use digitalisation to expand into new markets, offer new products, and create new types of value for customers, the public sector can now explore new opportunities to shape societal level impact. It's about pursuing different kinds of oppor-tunities, all made possible by new and extended uses of technology.

Enabling 21st century change

In this chapter we have looked at how we need technology to enable the work of the public sector, and the types of services and impact it can create. IT can no longer be just a department. Technology needs to be at the heart of every organisation's thinking. This also requires managers and leaders to understand its opportunities, potential, and limitations.

We have seen that organisations must be more flexible in how they approach technology, using loosely-coupled and Software as a Service solutions. We have considered how platform thinking can be extended much further. This is the opportunity for technology to reshape entire business models, extending the reach and impact of services.

The challenge for digital transformation is now to solve harder problems. This means that every organisation's long term goal should be to shift towards more integrated technology systems that enable new types of services and user experiences. In doing so they will be able to embrace new opportunities for more radical change to business models, and the ability to do more.

In part 2, we will move on to explore what good value looks like for the public sector. We will consider how organisations are creating new types of value, as well as delivering solutions faster and at lower cost.

Multiplied Thinking: Key takeaways from chapter 5

- **Make technology part of the DNA of your organisation.** The success of future digital transformation depends on how we select technology, how we manage it, and how we use it.

- **Deliver solutions with loosely-coupled technology.** Deliver more effective solutions with loosely-coupled architectures, such as microservices. Ensure that teams can integrate functionality seamlessly as services scale and adapt over time.

- **Build with common technology platforms.** Use Software as a Service (SaaS) solutions and tools as a means to collaborate more closely with other teams and organisations.

- **Extend platform thinking.** Explore how technology can help manage service demand and provide support with new business models – opening up roles and responsibilities for local communities and others.

- **Make the most of familiar technologies.** Recognise that existing technologies can lead to innovation and improved outcomes. Make the most of the tools people already use, and the potential to increase social connections.

- **Put digital transformation to work on harder problems.** Use technology to transform services in joined up ways, being prepared to do the hard work to deal with enterprise and legacy dependencies.

Part 2

Value

6 Value multiplied

In the second part of this book, we are going to focus on value. The aim here is to reset expectations for what good value looks like in the public sector, and the return on investment of the cost and time it takes to deliver digital transformation. This isn't just about making things cheaper or faster. It is also about our ability to do significantly more.

Much of the media coverage throughout the pandemic has focused on the large scale, top down programmes that struggled to cope, and not the thousands of smaller programmes delivering meaningful outcomes in communities across the country. While the costs of national programmes such as NHS Test and Trace have been widely reported, exceptional value has been repeatedly demonstrated elsewhere, in ways totally at odds with traditional public sector procurement and heavily specification based approaches.

When just some of the potential of technology and innovation is intelligently applied, the value that this can create is huge. Combined with inclusive design approaches, this is key to the impact the public sector can have. More should always be possible. Once we recognise this, the most important question we have to ask ourselves is "why not?"

The cost of change

Change has historically been expensive in the public sector, especially when involving technology. When we talk about the cost of change, we usually mean the time and money invested in the delivery of public services and policy as part of digital transformation.

But it's important to acknowledge that there are also human costs to consider, particularly when things go wrong.

When technology projects fail, it ultimately affects people. It is staff who must deal with the added stress and inconvenience of working with poorly designed or badly built systems. When technology fails to meet user needs in joined up ways, it's people that become a buffer. This leads to individuals having to put in additional work in order to simply keep our systems functioning. Unsustainable workplaces and staff burnout are common – in fact, a lack of adequate technology is a primary reason people choose to leave their jobs in the public sector. The most useful measure of value here is how technology removes administrative burden from people's work, but all too often it can be the other way around.

The cost of IT failures also affects citizens as much as those working to deliver services. A recent example of this can be found in reported underpayments of state pension – according to a 2021 report from the National Audit Office, outdated and unautomated IT systems contributed to 134,000 pensioners being underpaid by a total of £1 billion before April 2021.[95]

The public sector has a history of costly technology failures like this, and the way we measure value is partly to blame. Addressing this now is critical because of the continued human cost of poor outcomes in real life situations.

The measure of value?

When we think about technology, it's easy to fall into the trap of cheapest equals best value. But determining if a service or solution has simply been delivered more cheaply isn't a good measure of success in and of itself. In doing so we overlook what's created beyond the immediate costs of delivery time and effort.

A better measure of value is our ability to bring about outcomes more quickly and effectively. The main way to achieve this is through agile delivery.

Working in an agile way means building and iterating solutions based on what users need. In agile delivery, this is work that should be supported by data, and insights from regular user research. This way of working accepts that most teams will have a limited understanding of needs and requirements before they start. In these situations we always make some assumptions about what people need to do, or how we think that they will interact with a service or solution. And some of these assumptions will always be riskier than others, depending on the quality of our initial research and data.

As a 2015 blog post from the Government Digital Service (GDS) explains: "[agile] means spending money throughout the lifecycle of a service. Not throwing a lot of money at a project upfront, without knowing if it's going to be useful."[96]

This is an important point. Agile delivery requires governance whereby further investment is made over time as value is demonstrated.

In order to try and mitigate the risk of change, many organisations still try to specify every single requirement upfront in the process of building or buying technology solutions. This is over specification, which is then inevitably followed by longer and more expensive delivery cycles. It leads to poor user experience and outcomes, adding complexity to technology solutions that become difficult to manage, often with lots of unused features.

The over specification of upfront requirements is never likely to succeed due to how technology, circumstances and needs change. The reality is that flexibility is needed to make adjustments and shape requirements as work is delivered. This means acknowledging that there will always be a level of uncertainty to manage from the start of any work.

The British Army Jobs system

Unfortunately, there are still plenty of current examples that provide serious cause for concern in terms of the costs and time it takes to deliver technology based solutions. In these instances, we can directly compare the value being demonstrated with services that are supporting improved outcomes, faster, and at lower cost.

In December 2020, ten months into the Covid-19 pandemic, it was reported that a big four supplier had been quietly handed a £140 million contract with the British Army. This was an extension of its existing ten year contract, and part of a programme of work that had already committed to spending over £1 billion. The purpose of this work was to complete the delivery of a new recruitment system, including delivering the requirements for a new online solution – a process that had already suffered from serious technical problems and delays.

Instead of improving the Army's recruitment process, figures revealed in July 2020 showed that the new system actually lost the organisation 25,000 potential applicants in its first month alone.[97] A National Audit Office (NAO) report in 2018 also noted that the IT solution required manual workarounds for staff to process applications, as well as leaving candidates unable to manage their applications online.[98]

This is an extortionate amount of public money wasted. A new recruitment system built on modern technology by skilled experts and consultants shouldn't cost this much. It should certainly be capable of creating significant value and lead to improved outcomes, rather than declining numbers of applications and Army recruits.

We have highlighted this example not only because the costs involved are significant, but also because it illustrates other problems in how the work was approached.

Firstly, a specification led approach, or the problem of over specification is evident. The same 2018 NAO report states that the supplier underestimated the complexity of requirements, taking longer than expected to then develop a bespoke application. This points to a waterfall delivery approach, rather than a programme that was working in an agile way to deliver solutions more incrementally. Put simply: incremental delivery in an agile context means that successive versions of a product or solution add value. The focus is to deliver working software faster, with each successive version then building upon the previous, adding and testing functionality to ensure solutions meet users needs in the right ways as they are built and scaled.

The problem of over specification is also tied to another insight into the failure to deliver value. According to the NAO report: "Neither the Army nor their supplier tested fundamental assumptions they made before starting work." This is key. In this example, an important assumption was made before the project had started: that a centralised, automated approach to engaging with candidates, using a new online recruitment solution, would be the best way to increase efficiency and improve outcomes. Crucially, this turned out not to be true, with later research confirming that a more local and personalised approach was required for the successful recruitment of Army candidates. On the basis of this feedback from recruitment staff, the new system switched back to recruitment activities made available through local offices.

This insight could have been established cheaply, and quickly, by conducting user research with recruitment staff to test assumptions at the start of the project, before requirements were set, and before a line of code had even been written. But no one questioned the underlying assumptions being made about how technology was intended to transform the service. Years of effort and cost could have been avoided by simply talking to staff running existing services earlier.

Changing how value is demonstrated

The failures we have just described are linked to how supplier contracts are required (or not) to demonstrate value – which, as with our previous example, can take years from the start of a project to when solutions finally go live.

Much of the value that is realised from what the public sector spends is determined far in advance of the point of delivery, and is actually dictated by funding models. To stop escalating costs and the loss of billions of pounds of public money, it's appropriate at this point to suggest a solution: no single supplier contract should be worth more than £5–10 million at a time. Suppliers should be required to demonstrate value with this money before being given any further funding. This way the public sector should be able to generate far more value from the investment it makes in digital transformation. It would certainly prevent situations like the British Army Jobs example.

This represents the type of agile governance we described earlier. It is an investment in technology and delivery that's made over time, but only as the value of ideas and solutions is demonstrated. Assumptions have to be tested, and iterations made based on real user feedback. And, most importantly, the value of new products or services has to be represented, or measured as the result of change that people can see and experience for themselves.

Additionally, to support this funding model, there would also be minimum documentation standards and knowledge sharing requirements for suppliers. This could also include contractual commitments that ensure the use of open technologies and design systems as part of service delivery. With these things in place, different suppliers could pick up work seamlessly in the event of another failing to demonstrate sufficient value at any stage of delivery.

Comparing NHS Jobs

In direct contrast to British Army Jobs, a new recruitment platform for the National Health Service, NHS Jobs, was successfully delivered into a public beta over the course of 2 years, at an estimated cost of £11 million.[99]

The NHS is the world's fifth largest employer, and the new Jobs site was a replacement for older IT solutions which in 2019–20 handled 4 million applications per year for 380,000+ vacancies. The aim was to improve the recruitment experience, creating a system that would be more accessible and lead to more job applications. The team responsible for the work also wanted to better meet the needs of hiring managers with solutions that would be time and cost efficient, fitting seamlessly into their day to day.

The first live version of the service was delivered in just 18 months using incremental delivery, with design, testing and iteration to ensure that the right features and functionality were added to meet both citizen and staff needs. The risk of building the wrong solutions was managed through rapid prototyping and testing early in this process, testing key assumptions about how people would interact with the service, and how best to meet these needs. The team gradually increased their confidence in the solutions they were scaling through regular user research and eventually by working with live service data.

As this example shows, improved outcomes don't have to come at such a high cost. Digital transformation has already shown us that by using agile delivery and governance, we can deliver the same or more value in less time and at less cost than traditional IT contracts and specification led delivery approaches. The next time any government is prepared to invest £1 billion in technology and services, we should expect the value created to reflect and justify the level of investment. Much more is possible.

Reconfiguring to create value

It is said that Elon Musk came up with the concept for SpaceX on a flight back from Moscow in 2001, having been told that the price of buying a rocket was $8 million. He calculated that the raw material costs of a rocket were just a fraction of that price, so he decided to build his own rocket from scratch.

As Musk explained, "I tend to approach things from a physics framework [which] teaches you to reason from first principles rather than by analogy. So I said, okay, let's look at the first principles. What is a rocket made of? Aerospace grade aluminium alloys, plus some titanium, copper and carbon fibre. Then I asked, what is the value of those materials on the commodity market? It turned out that the material cost of a rocket was around 2% of the typical price – which is a crazy ratio for a large mechanical product."[100]

This is exactly the same first principles approach that involves breaking down and understanding the component parts of a system or solution, then reconfiguring them to create value. In the SpaceX example the ability to demonstrate value is aligned to a clear goal or business outcome – sending a flight into space at a fraction of NASA's costs.

This kind of thinking demonstrates our own need to be more ambitious. What might be possible through the value created by our public services if we were to apply the same type of approach?

Navigating complex systems with service design

Most services, along with the systems they're part of, are inherently complex. Since they consist of multiple interdependencies, there are many relationships to consider that shape how things work, how parts of services operate and how different types of needs are met. The key point about delivering value is focus. Good design that delivers value has always been about recognising and working within the constraints of time, budget and the size, complexity and interdependencies of services and the systems that they're part of.

Service design is a way of navigating complexity and applying first principles to our work. In service design, teams create artefacts such as service maps or blueprints as ways of understanding and working with the complexity of systems. This approach uses reductive models to break things down into their component parts, relationships and interactions in order to see what outcomes result from different journeys. All maps are purposely reductive in this way – a map of the world, for example, removes nearly every detail about Planet Earth to leave only relative masses, and names of countries and cities. But this is also what makes it useful.[101]

As we introduced in chapter 4, maps can help us to work with complexity as we design services at scale and deal with system level change. Clear visualisation helps us focus and align priorities. If you start with an "as is" view of a service or system, you can then visualise simpler models which can help to find user pain points, to identify quick wins and to create a shared understanding of where investment should be made in order to improve user experience and outcomes.

To give a specific example, in 2021 Hounslow Council created a detailed system map showing the different agencies involved in the care of children. This included mapping the data being collected and the systems being used to collect and manage that data. The "as is" view revealed to the team and the council that many existing services weren't joined up, while also highlighting the number of manual processes required to contact each agency to get updates on individual cases. This enabled the team to target changes and investment within the system that would create the most value. They were able to consider the potential for investing in new digital solutions and improved data sharing to enable and support agency partners. The mapping process also revealed what could be considered quick wins – such as improved content design and resources to support the immediate needs of social workers, parents and carers.

When working to identify and understand existing failure points within a system or service, user research can help to determine why this failure is happening and whether changes might add value in the short, medium, and long term. Part of this work involves avoiding short term fixes in isolation, pushing problems to somewhere else in a system, or moving existing costs between organisations and teams. Digitising existing processes, or applying new technology and tools, will not always be the right strategy. Such moves can actually increase costs within an organisation, or create fresh points of failure, if not designed with a clear understanding of context or staff and user needs.

By approaching change in this way, we can focus on the costs and dependencies of parts of a service or system. Just as with parts of a space rocket, we can interrogate the costs of technology dependencies and architecture, as well as staff costs and capabilities. Maps and frameworks that enable us to work from first principles also let us zoom in and out. Sometimes, the opportunity is to zoom right in to a single component of a system view – a single user interaction, touchpoint or technology choice. Other times, work that can deliver significant impact will require changes across a whole system, which we zoom out to identify.

First principles is an approach for reconfiguring public services and solutions. It's our ability to challenge and make underlying assumptions about the cost of change explicit. We can look more carefully at the time and the materials required to achieve a goal or to deliver an outcome that might have previously seemed out of reach.

Applying different lenses to change

As we have seen, it can help to break down large, overwhelming challenges into smaller parts with more achievable goals. By thinking about the specific parts of a system or service, and how they relate to one another, we can begin to understand the interactions between them and identify opportunities for change.[102]

This means working from first principles, and reconfiguring parts of a system and services to create value, but while also understanding the bigger picture of how policy, service and system relationships exist. A key part of this thinking is our ability to understand these interdependencies, and how different elements might need to be reconfigured in order to support improved outcomes.

As an approach to this TPXimpact has developed a framework to apply to digital transformation when working with change to systems in the public sector.

Each of the following lenses is an area of focus which staff in at least one organisation involved in the delivery of services have agency over. This allows us to examine where problems and change opportunities are and, when added together, these eight parts can be used to make up a whole system view:

- **Policy:** policy intent and how policy is being implemented, including the need for new policy or changes to an existing policy.
- **Operating models:** how services and business functions operate, including opportunities to add new channels and tailor models to be more flexible to meet individual needs.
- **Skills and ways of working:** the working and professional practices that support delivery, including how new skills and capabilities need to be developed to support new ways of working and delivery models.
- **Data:** how data is captured, managed, shared and used.
- **Governance:** how governance processes enable change, including how the organisation manages the risk of investing in opportunities.
- **User Experience:** user journeys and experiences determined by how services work and need to be accessed, including opportunities to meet changing user expectations and needs.

- **Content:** how information is designed and delivered, including as part of user journeys as well as content designed to support policy e.g. campaigns and marketing.
- **Technology:** supporting capabilities and digital channels, including opportunities to use technology in new ways to transform how services work.

Using these eight lenses helps us think about change in a specific area rather than immediately conceptualising what total change in all areas of a service might look like. For example, while a change to content alone won't solve system level issues, it will begin a process that shifts practice and perception in other areas. This can be the first step towards building momentum. It is the idea of starting small, but also thinking big. It means recognising value as something that has to be demonstrated in order to get buy in for new ways of working and further investment that can lead to even greater impact through digital transformation.

The distribution and extension of value

When we unlock value through efficiencies and improved outcomes, we must distribute the impact of this work equally through services that reach everyone.

We have already explored how change has been made possible during the Covid-19 pandemic thanks to teams and senior leaders focusing their time and investment on the most immediate problems. During this time we have often had to decide what is good enough given the constraints imposed by the pandemic and the need to respond to multiple urgent needs at once. In the book *Factfullness*, the late Swedish physician and statistician, Hans Rosling, makes this point, quoting his former mentor, Ingegerd Rooth, who had previously worked as a missionary nurse in Congo and Tanzania. "In the deepest poverty," she said, "you should never do anything perfectly. If you do, you are stealing resources from where they can be better used."[103]

This rule is applicable to every situation where resources (especially time and money) are scarce. When creating value through work that is publicly funded, it feels especially important to question how and where we're making investments and the impact this then delivers. Recognising where we can have the greatest impact is key. This is also a type of reconfiguring that means the distribution of value should reach much further.

What happens when a crisis affects everyone?

During the pandemic many people experienced challenging situations they wouldn't otherwise have had to consider. Covid-19 gave the majority of us a taste of the types of restrictions already experienced by sections of society, such as being unable to travel freely, and the burden of worrying about health and money.

It took a crisis that affected everyone for us to start solving problems that already existed for people living with a disability, or a dependency as a carer, cut off from services and support. When people talk of returning to normal, or even a new normal, we should consider how many people were excluded from society before March 2020, and look at how we can build something more inclusive than we were part of before. Add to this the fact that Covid-19 has created significant health and social inequalities which we have not yet fully come to terms with, and we can see that there is a lot to address.

Even with the pace of change increasing, the public sector does not yet fully deliver inclusive design that draws from the full range of human diversity, such as race, gender, disability and neurodiversity. Often, this adversely affects the standard of products and services for everyone.

There is a famous example of this in OXO Good Grips kitchen tools. The story goes that the handle of the OXO peeler is designed specifically to meet the needs of people with arthritis, but this actually means it's more comfortable and convenient to use for everyone. In the design film, *Objectified*, directed by Gary Hewitt, a designer involved with the original OXO design team notes, "What we really need to do is look at the extremes . . . If we understand what the extremes are, the middle will take care of itself".

In a design process, this is sometimes called looking at outliers, although it's really considering who is excluded by any type of design, and then using their perspective to create something better. Starting with the needs and the people we might have considered as outliers in this way becomes an approach to designing for everyone and, by doing so, extending value. If we want to follow this approach, we all have to do more to reach people who are excluded or disadvantaged, no matter what line of work we are in.

Focusing on diversity and inclusion enables us to create solutions that are more adaptable to everyone, and can be accessed and used in the largest possible range of situations. Kat Holmes was principal director of inclusive design at Microsoft from 2014–17. In her book, *Mismatch*, she notes, "Many inclusive innovations don't require a dramatic reinvention of technology. They don't require tearing down existing solutions to create new ones. Often, it's just applying a new lens to the resources that already exist, and forming new combinations of existing solutions. It starts by employing new perspectives to reframe the problems we aim to solve."[104]

For us, this is a combination of applying first principles and seeking new and closer perspectives as to how policy and services really impact people's lives. The goal is understanding and applying the value of new solutions in new contexts. *Mismatch* includes many good examples of technological design extending its value in this way. Take captioning: originally designed for the hard of hearing, captioning and subtitles have subsequently become essential tools for making information more readily accessible. In noisy airports and crowded pubs, people rely on captioning to access sports and news, and they're common in social media where users can't always turn up the volume on their smartphones. In a media world increasingly dominated by multinational streaming services such as Netflix, captions also open up drama from all corners of the planet, letting a viewer in Spain watch a programme made in Norway. This isn't a reinvention of technology, it's a reinvention of context, providing the opportunity to create more value from technology by understanding real life situations and circumstances.

To make sure the value we create is inclusive we must look beyond average use cases, user personas, and generalised users needs and requirements. It begins with our own teams, where we have to have diversity in order to find new perspectives. By then asking who might be excluded from our work, or by considering how to engage with those in communities who are hardest to reach, there is an opportunity to design in a way that extends more value to everyone.

Prepared to ask why not?

We started this chapter by considering the cost of change. We have seen that there are human costs to IT failures, as well as real and often escalating financial costs of delivery linked to technology in the public sector.

We have considered how value is created through reconfiguration, with the need to work from first principles, combined with the need to think bigger and be more ambitious. We have also compared different ways of working, and the importance of agile governance – supporting incremental delivery that can demonstrate value faster, and do so continuously.

To create better value for money, we will need increased efficiency in order to use public resources, time and materials more effectively. There must be no return to the huge IT budgets and overspends that neither improve outcomes nor represent value for money.

More value is about delivering responsibly and at scale, providing flexibility to the needs of people in different situations – using digital transformation to simplify and streamline how organisations operate, saving time and money.

In the next chapter we will look more closely at approaches to unlocking the value of technology.

Multiplied Thinking: Key takeaways from chapter 6

- **Reconfiguration makes more possible.** Focus on how people and organisations work together as part of systems, and how teams use, and are able to adapt technologies, capabilities and processes.

- **Measure value by more than cost.** A better measure of value is our ability to support change faster and more effectively. Invest time and money in more efficient ways that can ultimately lead to improved outcomes.

- **Work in an agile way.** Invest in work as value is demonstrated, ensuring teams and programmes don't get caught in the trap of over specification and upfront requirements. Be aware of the risk of untested assumptions.

- **Work from first principles.** Use service design, together with user research and technology discovery to understand and reconfigure how services work and can be improved.

- **Use different lenses to support change.** Understand relationships and interdependencies when working with complex systems, examining where the opportunities for change are – starting small, but also thinking big with a more connected, whole systems view.

- **Think about how value is distributed.** Use inclusive design approaches, focusing on diversity and inclusion. Create solutions that are more adaptable to everyone so they can be accessed and used in the largest possible range of situations.

7 Unlocking the value of technology

"The most dangerous phrase in the language is 'we've always done it this way.'"

– Grace Hopper[105]

We have already looked at how the public sector's relationship with technology needs to change. In this chapter we will look more closely at how we use technology to deliver public services. Starting with the right foundations, this is the need to make full use of technology when responding to future challenges, and in order to ensure that the impact of digital transformation reaches further into our organisations and society.

The potential benefits of technology mean that this is not the time to move slowly, and there is now a pressing need for more rapid experimentation. This includes how we adapt the use of technology in live service delivery – something we can reflect upon when looking more carefully at the sector's pandemic response.

The goal is to unlock the full value of technology through continued investment in digital transformation. But most of all, as technology continues to become increasingly accessible and affordable, this is the opportunity to improve outcomes much faster for people.

New possibilities

In 2021 the world lost the technologist Sir Clive Sinclair, who passed away at the age of 81. His ZX Spectrum computers were in large part responsible for creating a generation of programmers back in the 1980s, when the machines became best sellers in the UK and elsewhere.

He might not be as well known as Steve Jobs or Bill Gates but Sir Clive was a technology pioneer. When home computers were new and extremely expensive, he managed to bring them down in price through a combination of design and engineering, making home computing affordable and accessible to many households for the first time. As Sir Clive explained himself in a 2014 BBC interview: "We had to come up with a huge number of the innovations to get the price bracket where we wanted it." Early models therefore had their quirks. They were described as cost effective but a little bit strange. Their graphics suffered from colour clash and they had an unusual keypad design, moulded in one piece of rubber to make use of cheaper production methods.

Together with the price point of the technology the real innovation was programmability. With the ZX Spectrum, computers suddenly offered new possibilities, limited only by our imagination.[106]

We're sharing this example for two reasons. Firstly, for a sense of our shared history with computing and technology as a society. In the 40 years following the invention of the ZX Spectrum, home computing has reshaped our lives. Secondly, because just as with the possibilities of early computing, the biggest limitation to what's possible with technology today is still our imagination.

With the right approaches, technology can be configured in new ways, and with more flexibility than ever before. When we unlock the full potential of the tools at our disposal, this creates new possibilities for how we will be able to design services and deliver policy in the future.

Starting with the right foundations

In chapter 5, we explained how modern technology approaches use cloud computing to remove the complexity of having to host and maintain many elements of critical IT infrastructure. This gives us configurable computing resources – networks, servers, storage, applications, and services. An awareness of the benefits of cloud computing has grown over the past ten to fifteen years, as organisations have sought to become more agile, deliver greater value to their customers, and make their technology operations more resilient.

Yet although cloud adoption has increased, digital transformation is limited by the fact that many public services continue to rely on pre-cloud, legacy technology run from local data centres. These IT systems exist separately, meaning that it's difficult to get them to talk to each other and share information. This is why the personal details you might give to one part of government are asked for again by another part of government – or even another service run by the same department – leading to duplication of data and wasted time and effort.

Where cloud began as a way of providing faster, more efficient hosting of digital services, we now have public cloud ecosystems offering thousands of additional products, services and features. As well as providing the tools and platforms needed for a loosely-coupled technology approach, these promise advanced capabilities in the form of Natural Language Processing (NLP), Internet of Things (IoT) connectivity, Artificial Intelligence (AI), Machine Learning (ML), and edge computing. All of this can enable us to truly transform operations, respond to changing environments at pace, and deliver much greater value to taxpayers – but their value can only be unlocked through a strong base in cloud computing.[107]

This work is underway in many parts of the public sector, but not everywhere. In local government, the Local Digital Declaration now complements the Government's Cloud First policy which has encouraged more organisations to harness the power of cloud to transform services. Although digital transformation should not be driven by technology, the potential is to unlock the path to even greater benefits, while moving away from the high failure rates, security issues and poor user experiences provided by legacy technology.

We now need all of the public sector to build on the right foundations with modern cloud computing. This will enable us to fully realise its benefits, sharing information seamlessly between services, promoting collaboration across organisations, and transforming our work.

Inside out technology transformation

Until the Covid-19 pandemic, digital programmes were often undertaken as efficiency drives – with a rush to create the types of digitised solutions that have made transacting online faster and easier for many users, and cheaper for the public sector to operate. But technology also gives us many more far reaching opportunities.

As we described in chapter 1, much of what is considered successful digital transformation has largely been limited to improved digital interactions and user experiences on sites like GOV.UK. Meanwhile, real service outcomes – like access to financial payments or support – can still take weeks or months to process as they are dependent on legacy systems and inadequate technology.

True service transformation through technology now needs to happen inside our organisations. This is how we transform what happens backstage – the building blocks of how organisations work, how services are delivered, and how outcomes can be improved. It's only by transforming the relationship organisations have with technology that they can reimagine and deliver services in new ways.

What we are describing is inside out technology transformation, as it starts internally. This recognises that when we put the right systems in place, operational efficiencies and the flexible use of technology free up human time and allow organisations to work in new ways.

Increasing operational efficiency and productivity with automation

The primary way we can create operational efficiencies and improve productivity is through the use of automation, with technologies such as Robotic Process Automation (RPA), Artificial Intelligence (AI), and Machine Learning (ML).

Automation is the use of technology instead of people to do a job. It is created through the use of algorithms – sets of logical instructions, or rules, that a machine can follow.

As Hannah Fry notes in *Hello World: How to be Human in the Age of the Machine*, algorithms can be sorted into four main categories according to their function.[108] These are:

- prioritisation – making ordered lists
- classification – sorting, or categorising
- association – identifying relationships and finding links between things
- filtering and isolating – selectively removing information to focus on what's important, separating signal from noise

These functions enable the processing of large amounts of information quickly and accurately. Given a set of rules to follow and criteria to apply, technology can sort our data, help us prioritise work, and alert us when interventions are required, with important applications for our business and decision making processes.

Robotic Process Automation, for example, is the use of software to automate tasks such as extracting information from documents, transferring files and data entry. These kinds of tasks make up many repetitive, multi step processes that are both time consuming and mundane for staff, leading to poor job satisfaction, backlogs and potential errors. With RPA solutions, however, such tasks are accurately completed in seconds.[109]

RPA has applications across business and industry, with many organisations now exploring its benefits in their internal and external operations. As an example, the use of RPA at Morriston Hospital, part of NHS Wales, enables the specialist Medicines Homecare team to process patient prescriptions in a third of the time. By automating the review and validation stage of the dispensing process, pharmacists on the team no longer have to manually check each document individually, releasing vital time to spend with patients on the wards. With over 3,400 patients on its books, automation has provided much needed efficiencies for the Medicines Homecare service, whilst also ensuring medication is dispensed accurately.[110]

Although the exact definition of Artificial Intelligence is disputed, AI technology has a broader range of capabilities, meaning that it can be applied to a wide range of tasks and situations. AI functions typically display some level of automated decision making and problem solving ability, leading to more powerful solutions.

In machine learning (a subset of AI) computers are trained to complete tasks, so that they can then apply this experience to solve problems in new settings. Machine learning gives technology the ability to process unstructured data, meaning that it can work outside of rigid, rules based programming restrictions. Machine learning is core to the field of Natural Language Processing – which analyses our speech and is used in tools such as chatbots and predictive text – as well as common tools for pattern recognition such as search engines and the identification of images.

Such uses of technology have enormous potential in healthcare. In January 2020 it was reported that an AI program developed by Google Health could make breast screening more effective and ease the burden on the NHS where radiologists are in short supply. The AI had been shown to outperform specialists by detecting cancers that the radiologists missed, while ignoring features they falsely flagged as possible tumours.[111]

In more day to day processes, uses of automation with AI include tasks such as filtering harmful content online; using pattern recognition to detect potential fraudulent activities; and predictive analytics – finding patterns in data to analyse trends and inform policy and business decisions.

The most important consideration is that any application of AI must work with and complement human systems, tasks and decision making. When using this technology we should always apply certain conditions, such as understanding how decisions are being made, and putting transparent processes in place that are ultimately accountable to people. As the influence of technology grows across all our lives, getting the balance right between humans and machines is key.

The value of better technology for the people inside our organisations

Another goal of transforming public service delivery has to be providing great employee experience. When staff have access to tools that fully meet their needs, they can work more efficiently, with more flexibility to achieve their goals. As we have explored, technology also gives us the ability to remove repetitive tasks, freeing up time that can be focused elsewhere, and allowing support to be extended in new ways.

It is unfortunately still the case that staff plug the gaps in our public services when technology doesn't work well enough. Successful outcomes are achieved despite the technology teams are forced to work with, and in many instances – that they have to work around – in order to get tasks completed.

For example, it's still all too common for staff in places like the health system to spend up to 15-20 minutes having to log into IT systems at the start of the day, often with different ID requirements for the multiple systems they need to use.[112] There's evidence for this across the public sector, making it clear why productivity hasn't improved despite our increasing use of technology . . . Somewhere along the line in many digital transformation programmes, the idea of employee experience has been lost in the rush to provide better public facing digital solutions, even if staff are still stuck with the same old legacy systems.

Many technology solutions simply frame the public as customers and staff as secondary when it comes to user experience. We need to change this mindset – the people in our organisations need access to the right technology and tools if they're going to deliver more impact.

Every single person can be a multiplier with the right support and flexibility around their work. But the use of technology has been a contentious issue in the public sector for some time, with concerns about more open access to web based tools, and any kind of personal choice for staff around how they use technology as part of their job.

In 2016, the Ministry of Justice (MoJ) published a blog post stating that staff should expect technology at work to be at least as good as they have at home. As they explained: "Employees often have super fast wifi and the latest devices at home, but have to put up with creaking PCs and snail paced connections in the office. We want to provide technology that's at least as good as what they have at home, so they can work in modern, flexible and collaborative ways."[113] But even today, you will still find very different approaches to technology for public sector staff, with a range of policies around security and the use of devices, such as the ability to access your work email on your personal mobile phone.

The fact is that in many organisations, technology and software is still chosen by those that don't have to use it. The same problems exist with the technology that supports core business functions. As Sat Ubhi from TPXimpact explains: "I'm often asked which is the best customer relationship management (CRM) system to buy by local authorities. The challenge is that most are designed for commercial sales teams, rather than the needs of services teams managing customer data and relationships."

It is a theme that we keep revisiting, but part of the solution needed is flexibility. Even when moving to better and more open approaches to technology, particular solutions and software choices are still being forced upon teams and individuals. The reasoning for this is well intentioned, as it relates to the need to ensure solutions are secure, dependable and scalable, as well as an organisation's ability to provide support with monitoring and assurance processes. But great staff experience design needs to go further than this – it's about truly considering what a user needs to do, the decisions they need to make, and the actions they need to take – and supporting this workflow with flexible tools.

To make our organisations capable of delivering the most impact, it's essential that we now work more closely with employees to give them the best possible technology and software choices in order to fully meet their needs.

Even though many organisations fast tracked their migration to web based tools, more modern software, and virtual working solutions during the pandemic, we must recognise that digital transformation is a constantly evolving process. It should never be considered done, and the continuous revisiting of how well our staff systems, and solutions meet the needs of our teams is key to this.

Managing demand for services and support

One of the key pressures for public services during the pandemic has been demand management. Organisations have had to adjust rapidly to increased demand for support, whilst also adapting to new ways of working as the pandemic has shut down offices, and placed restrictions on front line services like the need to operate at reduced capacity.

Technology gives us the tools to manage peaks in demand and deal with service backlogs. In the NHS, where treatment waiting times have reached historic highs, many processes such as GP referrals and appointment bookings have always placed a significant administrative burden on hospitals. Doing this manually is extremely time consuming – particularly in Covid times – and it is unfortunately not uncommon for backlogs or processing delays to occur, ultimately impacting patient experience.

Wherever there are backlogs or significant demand for services, automation can help. This can ensure applications are processed more quickly, with additional information and advice also automatically sent out to users to support them as they wait to be seen.[114] This kind of automation acts as a way to manage the constraints of legacy systems, including a reliance on manual processes. However, automation also plays a central role in modern technology approaches, where it's used to scale services up or down according to demand.

Building services with a serverless approach, for example, out-sources the computer infrastructure that is required to build and run software applications to a cloud provider. This gives software engineers more time to focus on the code itself, as they don't have to worry about the infrastructure needed to host the code, the operating system, or compliance and security requirements. It means that when services receive more traffic, the cloud provider automatically allocates more servers to meet these needs. This automatic scalability has cost benefits too, as applications that are developed through serverless are typically consumption based, and only execute code when a specific event or trigger occurs. The advantage being that an organisation does not have to pay for an application when it is not being used.[115]

Universal Credit and digital foundations to support change

Universal Credit is designed to support people if they are on a low income or out of work. It includes a monthly payment to help with living costs and was introduced in the Welfare Reform Act 2012 as a means of bringing together six benefits, including housing benefit, working tax credits and jobseeker's allowance, within one scheme.[116]

At the start of the pandemic the UK government announced a furlough scheme where it would pay up to 80% of people's wages if their employer was affected by lockdown. This was later extended to some self employed workers, and, to provide additional support, the Chancellor Rishi Sunak also announced that the standard allowances of Universal Credit and the basic element of working tax credit would be increased by £20 per week to "strengthen the safety net" for individuals and families.[117]

Each of these announcements resulted in a spike in demand for the Universal Credit system. As a Department for Work and Pensions (DWP) Digital blog post in December 2020 explained: "The massive increase in traffic and claims that followed was highly unexpected and within a few months took us to 5 million active Universal Credit claims. We experienced a 40% increase in the initial weeks alone (up to 9 April), resulting in some spikes of a ten fold increase. In one particular fortnight we had 950,000 applications."[118]

Something that has largely gone unreported is how DWP was able to cope with this increased demand and went on to successfully implement rapid changes to the Universal Credit service and policy throughout the pandemic. This is a great success story for the Department after the challenges it has faced delivering such a significant piece of welfare reform in the past, with delays caused by the complexity of the Universal Credit policy, the scale of the rollout and the levels of organisational change needed.

DWP's ability to bring changes into effect quickly in response to a crisis was made possible through years of work before the pandemic to build a truly digital set of foundations with modern technology. After a difficult start due to outsourced technology contracts, since 2014 Universal Credit has been delivered with agile ways of working and multidisciplinary teams. These teams include a variety of roles, including Developers, Quality Assurance testers (QAs), Business Analysts, people from user centred design disciplines, Product Owners and Delivery Managers all working together. Importantly, teams also include people from business operations and policy, operating as a single service team. On the technology side the Department operates a platform that is hosted in a public cloud service, giving them the flexibility to manage demand on the system – using cloud hosting to scale up capacity on demand.

The Universal Credit policy itself, and the way it's financed by the government is a separate debate, but what is clear is that we now have a digitally enabled welfare system where changes can be made within days and weeks and not months. As Kayley Hignell, Head of Policy for Families, Welfare and Work at Citizens Advice explained after the more recent 2021 budget taper rate changes announced for Universal Credit: "We need a benefit system that can make quick changes like this to reflect the world around it. A strength of an in house digital system [is this type of flexibility]."[119]

Universal Credit is an example of the benefits of investing in in house digital infrastructure with work led by digital, design and technology specialists using agile delivery. This significant organisational change reflects a world where we should expect our systems and organisations to be able to respond to change and policy in real time, building on a foundation of modern cloud based technology infrastructure.

So far, we have focused on foundations and how technology can reshape our organisations from the inside out. The next thing we will consider is how we can identify and adapt new uses of technology. This is the opportunity to use technology in, as of yet, untested ways, helping us to rapidly adapt to changes happening in the world around us.

Unlocking value from technology

During the pandemic, the urgency of the crisis the public sector faced forced new types of experimentation with technology. As we highlighted in chapter 1, this was accompanied by an increased tolerance for risk in order to move fast and respond to immediate problems. Teams had to rapidly evaluate what was working, and what wasn't, as they built and scaled services and new digital solutions, some of which had to go live within weeks, or even days, of being commissioned.

What we start to class as experimental activities stand out because it's still relatively unusual to find the space for any experimentation as part of live service delivery. This is because most teams delivering services are also dealing with legacy constraints of internal policy, operational models and existing technologies, which then makes it hard to explore new ideas and opportunities.

If technology makes new models of the world possible, then we need ways to continuously adapt, test and learn about its uses. This is learning by doing. It is the belief that when facing uncertainty, the best way to respond is to rapidly prototype and test new ideas. Working in this way we can quickly build on what works, and move away from ideas that don't without investing more time and effort into them.

Keeping people connected when in hospital

How we use technology doesn't always have to be about inventing new tools, it can equally involve thinking creatively to apply what already exists in new ways.

For example, with friends and family not able to enter hospital wards during the pandemic, thousands of coronavirus patients were issued with iPads to communicate with loved ones. In the most serious cases, this technology enabled patients to say a final farewell. Early in the pandemic, independent projects such as "iComms for ICUs" were at the forefront of this work to crowdsource funds and distribute the technology.

Explaining the purpose of this initiative, Maeve Bradbury, the project's founder, told Sky News, "It must be so frustrating as a medic, when your job is all about making people better, but at the end, in very difficult, harrowing circumstances, you can't help them with that one thing they want more than anything else – which is to be able to talk to their loved ones."[120] As the project showed, getting iPads into hospitals was actually relatively straightforward thanks to crowdfunding and the support of community and volunteer based organisations.

Existing hospital wifi infrastructure also meant it was relatively easy to get devices up and running for patients.

The use of iPads in hospitals has evolved as the pandemic has progressed. Not only have they been used by hospital patients cut off from the outside world, they have also increasingly proved useful as a communication tool between medical staff, patients, and their families, for example, allowing patients to call nurses, and giving staff the ability to interact remotely with patients' families to provide updates.

A key learning is the role professionals play in the adoption and use of technology in real service delivery situations. In this example, iPads proved useful because medical staff were willing to make them a ubiquitous work tool. They've embraced the technology as part of their workflow, and have discovered ways to apply it to different situations.

However, even when there are clear benefits in applying technology in new ways, we have to carefully consider how and when it is used. Because just as new technology can be helpful, it can have negative effects or lead to unintended consequences. In a Sky News interview in May 2020, Dr Lucy Selman, a senior research fellow in palliative care from the University of Bristol, was asked about the use of technology such as iPads during the pandemic. Dr Selman said that while these connections could be a comfort of sorts, video calls replacing direct human interactions could also be very traumatic and not how families would want to say goodbye.

As with this example we can see how technology must be carefully integrated into care in order to add value in the right ways, and with consideration for personal needs and dignity. In these situations, processes should be led by front line staff as they are closest to how it can best be used and adapted to meet patient needs. What we are describing here is an extension of service design – in this case, the design and operational use of technology in front line services to meet staff and patient needs. Providing new tools and technologies can help front line services meet a wider range of needs, more effectively, but only when there is enough flexibility to let technology evolve with professional practice.

Making the space for experimentation

The type of innovation and change we're describing needs inside knowledge and expertise, but a great source of ideas can already be found inside the public sector if we're open to working with those closest to front line service delivery. As we have said throughout the book, everything we do should be centred on people, user experience and outcomes. But we must adopt approaches that directly involve practitioners — as well as end users – in the design of services, care and support. This is a way to benefit from their professional first hand perspectives, insights and experience.

One such approach is to set up dedicated service or innovation labs. This is where digital, design and technology specialists work directly alongside staff to identify and configure technologies to be trialled and tested as part of real service situations. This model can be delivered effectively as either short "design sprints" or as longer cycles of work – anything from 1-3 months to build, test and learn from new uses of technology.

TPXimpact worked with NHSX on a similar model in 2020, where as part of a three month series of delivery sprints we experimented with new tools and digital support for Children's and Young People's Mental Health services. Working with two local NHS Trusts as pilot sites, challenges included looking at opportunities for digital solutions to support children and young people in preparation for their first visit, and their subsequent treatment from Mental Health services.[121]

The first pilot site considered how technology could be used to design a more joined up process from the point of referral to initial assessment, including different communication touch points. The team worked from research insights highlighting that children, young people and families can feel disconnected, forgotten, or lost having to navigate the system after an initial referral – often uncertain about their next steps. They prototyped and piloted an automated SMS text message service so that young people could ask questions related to their assessment, and receive daily messages and updates along with useful resources over the waiting period after referral.

The second pilot site focused on testing a digital self referral service with a single front door concept. This was designed to address the significant waiting times that arose from disconnected referral processes, manual data entry and administrative tasks required within the system. Solutions were tested with GPs and health practitioners who had referred someone into children's and young people's mental health services in the past six months. Clinicians and partners found that the new online referral process gave them a tool that helped guide their conversations, bringing consistency across practices, and with the potential to provide a more constructive and consistent experience for service users as well.

This pilot work brought together clinical and operations staff within innovation lab settings, supporting the Trusts and NHSX to evaluate new uses of technology in order to support service pathways and meet user needs in new ways. By testing ideas with teams at local sites we were able to create sustainable changes to ways of working, empowering staff to use new tools – and giving them the confidence to experiment with technology – as well as growing organisational knowledge of user research and service design.

Giving front line staff the time and support to work with technology in new ways is a multiplier.

What we are describing is collaborative experimentation. This work requires support from a central team or dedicated digital resources, but most importantly, it must give people closest to service delivery the room to experiment with technology and changes to services in line with their own experience and expertise.

The ask is simply that people work openly and transparently in these situations, taking shared responsibility for the results, and feeding back on what works and what doesn't. This learning can then shape future models and solutions. Having a fully funded innovation or service transformation team provides the means to execute this process effectively, and to then build the tools for staff to use.

Exploring opportunity areas

Once an organisation is open to experimenting with technology and new ways of working, the question is what to focus on. Taking ideas from the examples we have looked at so far, teams could start by considering how digital transformation can be used to:

- change how people find, contact, or are referred into services
- support improved or simpler interactions and onboarding processes
- keep people updated with relevant information and notifications
- create new connections between people and information as part of a service
- make real-time adjustments to a service using data
- provide timely support when something goes wrong
- highlight the need for additional support, and interventions
- monitor for errors in systems and processes

This list describes what we can start to think about as individually targeted experiences, information and support. This is the potential to connect with people in new and more meaningful ways, tailoring solutions to their needs and preferences.

As we change our approaches to experience design, the next challenge is to think about how services work with, and can make better use of data. The decreasing cost of sensors and wearable technology that gathers and shares data is creating more potential for innovation, with new uses for "smart", internet enabled products emerging all the time. In areas like health, for example, an Apple watch now has fall detection which can call for help if you have an accident.

The growing sophistication of voice based tools and facial recognition similarly presents a range of opportunities, especially as we all become more familiar with this technology in our everyday lives. With the right support in place, there is now the need to experiment, testing and learning about what works in order to deliver benefits for both our organisations and citizens.

When experimenting with new types of solutions we must also carefully consider who will benefit from technology, and, more importantly, who it is most likely to exclude. This is the question of how far the impact of technology actually reaches, where the challenge is to design future services so that they can benefit everyone.

Building on new possibilities

Technology can help us move faster, reach more people, and organise more effectively. In this chapter we started by focusing on building the right foundations to unlock the value of technology in our organisations. We then looked at how it can transform our services from the inside out. This is about making digital transformation work harder and reach further. By changing the internal relationship organisations have with technology, we can also improve service outcomes.

In the public sector, technology has often been a set of constraints, reflected in situations like the tools and software we provide for staff. But with the right mindset, we can create a different story for the future of technology in our organisations. This is technology as a multiplier. It is a tool for us to experiment, working together with front line staff and users, and enabling services to meet changing needs and expectations.

In the next chapter we will look more at the importance of data in how we transform public services and future policy.

Multiplied Thinking: Key takeaways from chapter 7

- **Build on the foundations of modern cloud computing.** Public cloud ecosystems offer thousands of options that can be configured to service needs, transforming operations.

- **Transform services from the inside out.** Unlock value and support human interactions with automation and increased operational efficiency and productivity.

- **Prioritise employee experience.** Give people better tools to support their work and priorities, with the flexibility they need to improve services and outcomes.

- **Recognise that context creates value from technology.** Enable professionals to shape how they use technology as part of front line services.

- **Invest in experimentation.** Create and fund experimental spaces, teams and projects to test and evaluate new uses of technology transformation through delivery.

- **Understand the impact of technology choices**. The value of technology has to be evenly distributed. Question who will benefit, and, more importantly, who is most likely to be excluded.

8 Being bolder with data

Data is essential to realising the public sector's ambitions for digital transformation. It is how we capture, organise and quantify information and signals about human activities and behaviour, including the environment around us.

In this chapter, we will look at how data can help us to design solutions that meet needs in new ways, as well as delivering better outcomes. While data is already used as a tool to guide policy making and service delivery – with analytics helping us understand service usage – feedback and reporting cycles in the public sector are traditionally slow, taking weeks, months or years. This is in direct contrast to the real time data operations of many modern businesses.

Although there are cultural and governance challenges to overcome, we have the opportunity to unlock the full potential of data in the public sector. In doing so data can act as a multiplier – supporting how we deliver solutions which meet citizen and organisational needs more quickly and effectively. This requires bolder thinking, but it's data that gives us the ability to extend the impact, flexibility and reach of future services and solutions.

The value of data sharing

Many of today's largest and most successful businesses have seen spectacular growth fuelled by their focus on creating exceptional customer value through data. Tech giants like Amazon, Apple, Facebook, Google and Microsoft all collect and analyse huge amounts of data about their users, applying these insights to create and improve the value propositions of the products and services they offer.

These companies all collect and use data within their own ecosystems. If you're an Apple customer, for example, your products and services will be linked through devices including your iPhone, Apple Watch, and Apple TV, as well as many other touch points – all of which collect and share data about you. This gives Apple the insight they need to create user experiences that feel personal to you, connecting their products in a seamless and joined up way, while also targeting you with new products, services and content based on your preferences and behaviours.

The potential for companies to keep creating additional customer value with this level of detailed data insight is significant. However, despite our expectations for modern internet enabled services, this use of our data by the private sector is not typically transparent, with individuals often unsure as to how their information is being collected, stored, and ultimately sold.

The public sector clearly has much to gain from being bold with how it collects, uses and shares data. Government organisations already operate their own ecosystems, with countless large data sets covering everything from citizen financial information to public infrastructure, representing the lives of the entire UK population as well as our natural and built environments, and economic activity. Just like the data driven insights businesses gain from their products, this opens up the potential for detailed insights into public services and policy, ultimately leading to better outcomes for citizens.

Although the public sector can take inspiration from the ways many modern businesses use data, it must also do much better than the private sector. The opportunity is for our public institutions to be data leaders. This means being at the forefront of reimagining society's relationship with data, how individuals own and consent to their data being used, and setting the standard for ethical approaches which should ultimately lead to better outcomes for citizens.

The existing relationship we have with data

When we're considering the future of public services it's important that we start by acknowledging that culturally and historically, the UK has rejected data accumulation and cross agency sharing amid fears of excessive control, data leaks and potential abuse. The government's National Identity Cards scheme, for example, was axed in 2010 partly due to expense but also due to concerns that it infringed the civil liberties of individuals.[123]

While it might sound like an ideal solution, the use of a single identifier across all government services carries a lot of risk. National Insurance numbers, for example, could in theory be used to identify working people and connect their records across different systems. However, if joined up, this would allow for all sorts of unexpected links to be made from their employment to their health and financial data. National Insurance numbers are also unreliable. Many organisations have managed this data for decades and as a result there are gaps and misallocations – not everyone has a National Insurance number, some people have more than one, and there is no single database which holds all of this information.[124]

The reality is that data in the public sector sits mostly in its own protected silos, be they teams, specific tools or individual systems within separate organisations. Driving details are stored by the Driver and Vehicle Licensing Agency (DVLA), criminal records by the police or prison service, and even within a hospital, a patient's administrative data might be kept on a different system – maybe even only accessible on a different computer – from their X-ray images. If you happen to find yourself in an NHS hospital any time soon, doctors won't necessarily have direct access to information from your previous visits, or information from the consultations you've had with your GP.

This level of fragmentation in how data is stored means that organisations and teams looking to use data in new ways now need to work to link it together. This is a particular challenge where there is a lack of agreed data standards and governance – and as we saw with National Insurance numbers, it may never be practically feasible with some kinds of data. We can add to this a further complication in the fact that many commercial technology solutions lock in data, making it hard to extract. The need for a more connected approach to data sharing goes hand in hand with the investment the public sector now needs to make in modern IT systems, with well managed Application Programming Interfaces (APIs) that make data more accessible.

How a lack of data sharing impacts front line services

The scenario of services, systems and local support infrastructures not sharing data is very common. You can see it clearly in most front line services – in the intersection of health and social care, for example – and especially where there are dependencies on third parties.

In 2018, TPXimpact worked in North East Lincolnshire to review Adult Services as part of ongoing work to bring together health and social care.[125] All of the service users we interviewed described how they had to repeatedly provide the same personal information when being referred between services in the region. This left people feeling frustrated and isolated from services that seemed to know nothing about them. To directly quote one person's experience: "They don't know me or my case . . . they didn't know who I was or what I was talking about when I tried to ask [about my situation]. Services do not communicate with one another."

This type of experience, of passing through a system feeling invisible or unheard, is far from ideal. It is a good example of how more joined up approaches to data can ensure everyone has meaningful, personal interactions with any system providing care – with councils and providers able to go beyond simply meeting statutory requirements for care, and making sure that people have a more positive experience when receiving this type of support.

With the right investment in modern technology approaches – including cloud computing solutions – the ability to share data and make systems interoperable should now be achievable for most organisations.

This is also the opportunity to rework process heavy systems into more flexible, outcome focused services supported by data. Depending on service architecture choices, this might require wide ranging or incremental changes to technology solutions. But with a focus on user needs, many systems used to support services in areas such as Adult Social Care can be transformed through the use of APIs, giving users the ability to access and interact with data in real time.

Data sharing is more than a technology problem

When we look into the reasons why data isn't being shared across teams, departments, and partner organisations, it becomes clear that technology is only part of the issue.

In North East Lincolnshire, the biggest problems were being caused by the siloed working of organisations in the region's Adult Services system. Care providers weren't always open to handing over information about individual cases, which made creating the best care plan for each person a difficult task as they moved through the system. This lack of data sharing was connected to trust, and how risk was perceived. With no framework or clear accountability around data, this made it risky for staff to share data outside of their own organisations.

To resolve this the council was able to work with its local Clinical Commissioning Group, and eleven providers, putting in place a strategy for data governance – shared agreements to determine how data could flow between all parties within a system – for both the benefit of service users and staff. In this example, appropriate governance to increase data sharing included the adoption of new data quality standards for all providers to follow. This was also supported by the creation of sharing agreements between staff and providers that linked their work more effectively.

Importantly, in situations like this, data governance ensures that every organisation is working within the law on data protection and privacy. Currently the European Union General Data Protection Regulation (GDPR) framework covers how UK organisations are required to work with personal data. Handling personal information as part of public service delivery remains important and complex, and it's essential that organisations, as well as their suppliers or other external providers, understand their roles as data processors or as data controllers. It's also essential that the public sector goes beyond compliance and sets the best possible example around sharing the smallest amounts of information needed to be practically useful, while anonymising data and securing data to protect individual privacy.

Making data central to design

When there is a data and information sharing problem to solve within services, we need to start with an understanding of how people experience these systems and what their needs are. To do this effectively, we must also involve those delivering services to find out how data can help them to best meet the needs of the people they are supporting.

The requirement in most scenarios is for health and care professionals to understand someone's personal story so that they can provide the best possible care. Any data they are given, such as results or reports, should support their face to face assessment of the individual. But even with good (or improved) data sharing in somewhere like the NHS, many consultants only have minutes to review a new case before they meet the patient face to face.

This, then, is the challenge. If and when more data is shared, how can it be used to meet a person's needs if the consultant doesn't have any more time than they do now? As we explore how data can create more value, we know it can't be about reducing human interactions to a transactional, impersonal exchange of information.

Instead, whenever we design for how and when we use data, it must be with an increasing contextual awareness of real needs and situations. The problem to solve isn't in data gathering, it's in data presentation.

In the context of a specialist consultant, too much data presented in the wrong places or at the wrong times could be unhelpful, or even harmful. But the right data, in the right format, will support the information the consultant is able to get from the patient first hand, enabling them to demonstrate their understanding of that person's context, understanding their history and building a positive relationship.

As Christian Madsbjerg, a professor of Applied Humanities, explores in his book *Sensemaking: The Power of The Humanities in the Age of the Algorithm*, "In a bureaucratic system, data is very abstract – mostly numbers and reports . . . The data is well done technically, but it's very hard to get any feel for what kind of human situation underlies the documents. What is really going on for people?"[126]

We need data to be central to how we design for human interactions, and, in this particular example, how care is delivered. Design also has to be central to how we present data, making information useful and adaptable – representing real life situations and needs rather than abstract information. This is essential if we are to make more use of personal and shared information to support individual needs and outcomes.

Data insight and targeted support

In order to deliver the most value from the people and resources at their disposal, organisations require quality data insight to gain an accurate picture of who requires support and the kind of support this should be. For organisations such as local government, housing associations and citizens advice teams, their priority has always been to reach people with the most urgent needs. This relies on being able to translate data into action quickly.

In 2020, Camden Council developed Beacon – a digital solution for multi agency data sharing – giving the council and their partners in the voluntary and community sector a single view of residents. By capturing resident needs in one place, council staff could connect them directly to appropriate support – such as those distributing food packages and medicines to people shielding at home during the first lockdowns of the Covid-19 pandemic.[127]

Data sharing was central to the design of the new system, as speed and simplicity were vital for council staff delivering in a crisis. Whereas previously staff had manually copied and pasted data from spreadsheets, for example, the new solution automated the prioritisation of individuals most in need.

Putting data at the heart of their approach allowed the council to move beyond a basic understanding of people's needs to deeper analysis of the underlying issues. If a resident asked for a food package, for example, the data was there to tell them why – building a picture of that person's social and financial circumstances, and identifying opportunities for further support. Additional needs identified ranged from people socially isolating needing someone else to walk their dog, to a number of more complex situations that required referrals to services such as housing or children's and social care teams.

Since launch, Beacon has supported staff to manage and prioritise their entire caseload, reducing the time spent on manual tasks, improving overall data quality and giving them more time to spend with people in need of help. Over 3,000 people on the Camden NHS shielding list had been successfully contacted and triaged.

Increased use of data in service delivery

The pressures of the pandemic have caused more organisations to ask practical questions about how they should share data, handle data governance, and future proof their data approaches to keep up with technological change. In government there is also a growing and shared ambition to do more with data.

The Government Digital Service (GDS) 2021-2024 strategy states the need to put data at the heart of a strategic approach, which means "being able to comprehensively understand how people interact with the government online, and being able to use data about people and government (with permission) to provide the level of service that they expect."[128] This could signal a huge change from the UK's history of siloed data approaches, with real benefits for citizens, as the strategy sets out a clear priority to create "joined up and personalised experiences of government for everyone".

We know that a key point of failure in existing services is the time people have to spend deciphering content and navigating information in order to complete tasks, or even just to find the right place to start. We now have the potential to remove this type of friction with better use of data, ensuring that all the information and support people receive when accessing public service is relevant, targeted and useful in supporting the outcomes they need.

With these changes GDS are actively exploring how to enable departments to share information about users across other parts of government. This includes scenarios such as "tell us once", where people could report commonplace changes to circumstances, like moving home, and their records would be automatically updated across different government systems. This would prevent duplication and errors, as well as the need for users to change their details multiple times with different departments.

Departments are also setting out their own intentions to make data the primary tool in shaping service delivery. The Home Office, for example, stated in its latest technology strategy that: "By transforming the way we think about architecting our systems, we'll make data central to the design. We will focus on how we use and maintain data sets, using data models, metadata and data standards wherever possible."[129]

Data as a multiplier

We have already seen examples of how data is a multiplier. This includes how data sharing makes more personal, targeted support and experiences possible. Whilst the ambition being shown by government around how future services use data is welcome, greater ambition is needed. We have to think bigger.

To be bold with data, we must now move away from the risk averse mindset that has prevented data from being shared outside individual teams and across organisations. The opportunity cost of not sharing data now outweighs the risks of making it more openly accessible – providing effective data governance is in place.

Currently, however, combining different data sets can be difficult. As Deven Ghelani, founder of Policy in Practice explains: "When you link or map data on to each other, you need to go through lengthy governance processes with the owners of that data. Say you want to track the relationship between poverty and children who end up in the care system – you need agreement from the heads of child services and revenues and benefits to make that happen."[130]

Along with the personal data it holds on citizens, and the information it gathers from interactions with its services, the types of data sets available to the public sector are wide ranging. They include everything from Unique Property Reference Numbers (UPRNs) held by the

Ordnance Survey to identify addresses; to information from institutions such as the Office for National Statistics (ONS) which can tell us about the economy, population trends and our communities; and the National Archives, which holds data on the legislation underpinning particular government services.

To realise its full value, public sector data like this must be opened up and used more widely. By making data sets accessible to teams and organisations with legitimate interests, we can generate meaningful insights. This will be critical to how we meet the future needs of citizens as well as unlocking the potential for new types of innovation.

Opening up population scale data

By opening up population scale data, interested parties can be given the building blocks for new products and services.

In 2007 Transport for London (TfL) took this approach when it started its open data initiative, releasing static data around train and bus timetables.[131] This led to the creation of hundreds of transport apps, and an ecosystem of innovators finding new ways to improve the lives of citizens, as well as boosting the city's economy. TfL now presents its data sets via a unified API, which provides real time information on everything from air quality to tube service status, and is designed for applications to use at scale.[132]

The Citymapper app is an example of the positive results of this approach, as it is the kind of digital tool most Londoners now take for granted to travel as seamlessly as possible around their city. This type of innovation also benefits public sector organisations themselves, as they then have the opportunity to make use of such solutions as part of their own cloud based, loosely-coupled technology approaches.

Increasing expectations for real-time services

As part of the digital interactions we have with modern services, more of us now expect the kinds of joined up experiences that make use of personal data. Increasingly, people will have the same high level of expectations for all of their interactions with the public sector as they do elsewhere. This is the expectation that organisations reuse data without inconveniencing the end user by asking them to provide the same information more than once. It is also the expectation that data is used intelligently to make experiences more tailored to individual needs and preferences, helping people to achieve their goals in the fastest, simplest way.

In his 2018 blog post *Real-time government*, Richard Pope described how one of the main characteristics of modern digital services is that they all operate in real time. If you want to buy something on Amazon, for example, you see if it's out of stock immediately. Pricing on Uber similarly responds to demand in real time, so you pay more when there are fewer drivers available. However, unlike these businesses, users are typically unable to interact with government services in this way.

As Richard explains, in government, data still "tends to be copied and shared between and within organisations using overnight batch processes, rather than accessed via APIs. Fundamentally, the infrastructure and the data hygiene does not exist for government to systematically operate in real-time."[133] To get to this point there is an immediate need to move away from slow data reporting cycles, transform our technology systems and to put in place more rigorous data practices. This is an ongoing process, but it must involve ensuring data is up to date, free of errors and duplication, and held in standardised formats.

Moving towards smarter services

So where do we need to be bold? The idea that data can be used to identify patterns and behaviours, with systems capable of responding in real time has enormous potential. It represents a new generation of smarter services – where people are able to track the exact status of an application they've made in a government system; where they can see changes to their patient pathway using real time healthcare data; and where services in our local communities are capable of responding to the environment around us – like councils monitoring pollution levels across a local area, and providing on demand public transport solutions to reduce traffic.

Technology capable of identifying patterns and behaviours also has huge potential to give local authorities and their partners the tools to transform how front line services like care are delivered. Many councils and housing associations have already installed smart home devices that are capable of monitoring whether a fridge door has been opened, or identifying the last time a kettle was boiled. These solutions build up a picture of typical daily activity and can alert staff to situations where people could be at risk – supporting carers and improving outcomes for individuals in their homes.

The future of personal data ownership

Where the public sector should act differently compared to the private sector is in its approach to the ownership of personal data. As we consider the better use and wider opening up of data, we also need to empower citizens to own their own data and to offer it up on request. This type of transaction needs to be clear about how data will be used, and it should also be clear how sharing data will benefit the user, giving them full control over what is shared, where, and with who.

We can start to consider how the public sector could take the lead in changing the model of data ownership, and who profits from the data created when individuals use services. Ideas like Web 3.0 – a decentralised version of the internet based on blockchain technology – envisage a future where citizens would not only be able to create and access information online through the types of browsers, services and social media platforms we use today, but where they would also own and control this data.[134]

The concept of decentralisation in technology is interesting as it distributes control across a system or network. Unlike the centralised digital services we are familiar with today, where one single authority sits at the heart of the system, decentralised systems are controlled by all members of a network equally. We might be some years away from realising the full potential of decentralised technology and data approaches, but there are some current examples. The Estonian government, often celebrated as having created the first truly digital society, already uses blockchain technology to ensure its networks, systems, and data are private and secure for its citizens.[135]

Back in the UK, a more recent example of data centralisation has played out very publicly through the development of Covid-19 contact tracing solutions enabled by bluetooth technology. In 2020 the government initially persisted with their own approach to custom building a smartphone app using a centralised data model. In this NHS app, contact matching took place via a central database, giving the government direct ownership of the identity data collected from people's phones. Even though this data was anonymised, restrictions on Apple and Android devices prevent this kind of centralised data gathering due to privacy concerns, and during a pilot on the Isle of Wight the app struggled to identify other phones it came into contact with. This eventually led the government to scrap the project in favour of a decentralised version that uses Apple and Google's software, where data about people's interactions is stored on individual phones.[136]

The story of the Covid-19 contact tracing app is a good example of the data privacy issues the public sector faces if it is to make better use of data in both policy making and service delivery. Because although millions of UK citizens have voluntarily used the decentralised contact tracing app during the pandemic, this was in response to a specific set of circumstances – the urgent need to control the spread of the virus.

Other data sharing initiatives have been much more controversial. The decision taken by the NHS in 2021 to open up GP patient data for planning and research purposes, known as GPDPR, was met with wide public protest as people became aware that their data would be shared without their permission.

As the contact tracing app and the lack of communication around GPDPR shows, people are more likely to consent to sharing their data if they are properly informed about its purpose. The sharing of GP data may have been a route towards improving medical outcomes, but users were not appropriately informed, leading to GPDPR being deferred by the NHS to provide more time for consultation with patients, doctors, health charities and others.[137]

Public expectations for data ownership, privacy, and sharing will continue to evolve rapidly as our relationship with digital technology changes, and when specific circumstances change. Most importantly, accountability for data, and how the public sector uses it, has to be connected to an understanding of real citizen needs and behaviours, ensuring that this enables us to continue to ask questions around privacy, safety and consent, always putting people and their needs first. Any increased use or sharing of data will need to protect individuals and public institutions, with information accessed only by those who need to use it. In this way, opening up data from existing silos should not compromise privacy since only the required information would be released with permission, and only in a highly anonymised form when appropriate.

Increasing data maturity across the public sector

In order for organisations to be bolder with how they use data, what we are advocating for is the need for increased data maturity.

While improving how the public sector captures, stores and uses data sounds like an achievable goal, this ignores the fact that existing data isn't necessarily in any kind of digital format. Before organisations can start to address how to create high quality data solutions, there is the significant task to consider of formatting physical files, along with how to deal with data stored on ageing legacy systems. Migrating physical data is a challenge as it depends on how long that data needs to be held, and there is also the need for organisations to stop copying data in ways that results in out of date, poorly managed information stored across multiple organisations.

The answer here isn't the creation of large centralised data stores. What we need instead is more interoperability, and the adoption of shared data standards across the public sector. This will mean that data can be better managed, maintained and joined up effectively from local data sets, with APIs providing access to data so that providers know who has access and can ensure they keep an up to date version of information at all times. With the right accountability and permissions users then stay in control of what happens to their data, and who really benefits from it.

Most of all, we need organisations that are prepared to invest seriously in how they manage and use data, ensuring that they have the expertise they need to work in new ways. The result of this should be brilliant quality data, and data management at every organisation level, including both department level and locally.

Data maturity in our organisations needs to grow from this foundation. It means getting the basics right with data integration and validation so that information is in a system once, accurately and in the correct format. Maintaining quality data in this way will also then help us to remove the constraints of organisational silos, eliminating duplication and errors.

Moving towards data excellence

The first step towards increasing data maturity in any organisation is leadership. Creating a mature data culture begins with helping everyone to understand the importance of data and the need to make it more freely available – as opposed to it being owned in silos or separate business units. Any organisation must then become more proficient at data use through investment in:

- **Data skills:** The ways of working, tools and approaches needed to embed data science into policy, operational, and delivery teams.
- **Data governance:** The management of data assets.
- **Data discoverability:** How people inside and outside of an organisation can find useful data.
- **Data integrity:** The level of trust in data and insights being maintained and created.
- **Data driven insights:** The ability to identify patterns from data, informing policy, interventions and service based decision making.
- **Data driven feedback loops and actions:** The ability to learn and measure progress, using data to track progress against key metrics.
- **Data security:** The ability to protect data and personal privacy, allowing for individual permissions and ownership of data.

As an example of this type of investment, we can look at the national charity, Citizens Advice, which is an organisation investing in appropriate structures and approaches to managing its data.

Citizens Advice creates large volumes of unstructured data through its work supporting clients – the people who contact them online, over the phone or face to face. Applying Natural Language Processing (NLP) to this data enables the organisation to automatically analyse what people are telling support staff. This makes it possible to quickly identify trends in the issues people are experiencing, informing service and policy decisions as the organisation works out ways to meet these needs. The creation of a mature data culture at Citizens Advice has also included staff training, giving everyone a clear understanding of their responsibilities around data, including its ethical considerations.[138]

The type of data maturity we have just described now needs to be reflected across the public sector in how every organisation uses data to deliver the best possible services and support – informing how it works, and how it makes decisions.

This is about creating value through how organisations meet people's needs and deliver improved outcomes. But most of all, better use of data should work for the benefit of every citizen. It is the opportunity for our public institutions to become leaders in ethical, open uses of data that support innovation, and make new types of change possible for the next generation of public services.

Things could be better – a lot better

In this chapter we have looked at how we need to be bolder with data. This means opening up data more widely inside and outside the public sector, but while ensuring people have control over their personal information, determining who has permission to use it, where they will use it, and for what purpose.

We have seen how data sharing is more than a technology problem. We have also seen first hand how data enables us to design entirely new services that can target support and enable a more holistic approach to meeting people's needs. This makes the most of meaningful collaboration between the voluntary and community sector, and government, extending the reach of local services and support.

Making data central to the design of services, we can now meet the changing needs and expectations of citizens, while enabling the innovation needed for future challenges.

In the next chapter we will look at how we can make more possible from delivery, including the approaches we might take when designing and building future services.

Multiplied Thinking: Key takeaways from chapter 8

- **Support data sharing in front line services.** With modern technology approaches data sharing is now achievable for most organisations, but this also requires changes to ways of working and governance to succeed.

- **Make data central to design.** Focus on data presentation as well as data gathering. Work with data in real life situations, using data insight to target support where needed.

- **Open up data.** Make population scale data sets accessible to teams and organisations with legitimate interests. This can then generate meaningful insights and unlock the potential for new types of innovation.

- **Move to real-time, smarter services.** Use data to identify patterns and behaviours, with systems capable of responding to user expectations and needs in real time.

- **Consider the future of data ownership.** Look at how citizens can be empowered to own their own data and to offer it up on request using decentralised technology.

- **Invest in data skills and experience.** Ensure that there is appropriate data governance, discoverability, and data integrity in your organisation. In order to be bolder with data, we now need all organisations in the public sector to increase their data maturity.

9 Making more possible from delivery

> *"I was attracted both by the sheer idea and the fact that it had never been done before"*
>
> *– Margaret Hamilton*[139]

In a world of complex systems and public services, it's delivery that shapes the environment our teams work in, and the success of the work they undertake. This is how work gets done, the structures and support we provide to our teams, and how they are enabled to create solutions in iterative ways using modern methods and tools. Combined with how we use design, technology and data, it's delivery that helps us to put new ways of thinking and approaches to how we work into practice.

In this chapter, we will look at how to make more possible from delivery. We have seen how the public sector's pandemic response pushed teams to act quickly, with clear changes to delivery. In some cases this involved breaking away from established approaches in digital and change programmes.

Teams delivered incredible results in this period, sometimes achieving more in a short space of time than we might have thought previously possible, even building solutions in a few days or weeks. While there is no need for delivery methods to return to pre pandemic ways of working, the challenge is to find delivery approaches that continue to question what is possible, shaping how our teams respond to future challenges in a sustainable way.

What's not been done before

For Margaret Hamilton, the trailblazing computer scientist in charge of the software supporting the successful NASA Apollo 11 mission to land on the moon, it was the sheer idea and scale of something that had not been done before that attracted her to become part of this effort. Everyone she worked with – from engineers to human computers, scientists and administrators – needed to play their part, demonstrating time and again that with the right expertise and mindset, complex problems could be solved, and previously undeliverable outcomes could be reached.

This is an example that demonstrates the importance of teams working together to deliver shared goals and outcomes. It highlights the need to carefully organise how teams work, assigning specific roles and responsibilities, and ensuring the right blend of experience and skills is supported by a productive environment. Put simply, team structures and support are essential to the success of any piece of work.

It is also the size and ambition for what can be accomplished that motivates teams to achieve their goals. In chapter 3 we talked about the importance of the vision we set out to work towards. We now have to be prepared to take our own moonshots, asking much bigger, more fundamental questions about what can be achieved through the approaches we take to delivery.

The future of digital delivery

When considering future delivery approaches, the important thing is to continue to build on what we already know works, using agile delivery methods, user centred design and research, and applying best practice for developing and testing technology solutions.

We can then apply new thinking. This includes how we optimise for more ambitious work and goals, work creatively, and organise teams in new ways.

Building on the delivery methods set out in GOV.UK and NHS guidance and service standards, teams have already been working in much more flexible ways over the past decade, continuing to make adjustments throughout the pandemic. Key changes to how delivery is evolving include:

- **More flexibility around phases of work:** Discovery-Alpha-Beta-Live delivery cycles are increasingly being applied in more flexible ways. While teams outside of central government were already adapting delivery phases to meet local needs and contexts, this has been made even more apparent with the need for organisations to deliver live solutions faster during the pandemic. Many teams are also specifically rethinking approaches to discovery – how they learn about user needs and frame problems to solve. The challenge is how this now transitions into all phases of delivery.
- **Building with shared capabilities and solutions:** Delivery approaches have become increasingly focused on identifying and building with shared capabilities and platforms, including Government as a Platform (GaaP), and working with cloud based technologies. Teams are becoming less dependent on building bespoke solutions, especially with the success of shared services like GOV.UK Notify, and with open source practices. With more digital solutions being delivered to the same service standards, the potential for reuse has increased. Local government initiatives like

LocalDrupal – a shared web publishing platform now adopted by 22 councils – also means more organisations are working together and benefitting from shared solutions.[140] The increased use of Design Systems is also helping teams to reuse work that has been designed and tested elsewhere.

- **Working with real-time services:** Delivery approaches are increasingly aligned to working with live service data and in live operational situations with front line teams. There is now a slow move away from the siloed, fixed, linear solutions that were the result of earlier digitisation work, and towards services that are more responsive to different contexts.

- **The transformation of whole services:** Where the remit of digital delivery has increased, this now includes design for both digital, and non digital parts of services. It also recognises that the transformation of user journeys and outcomes requires the involvement of different organisations and other delivery partners. This is still the biggest challenge in government – with few examples of entire services and supporting infrastructure being built in a digital first way. Where this is happening, we have already highlighted how it has helped policy areas and services like Universal Credit to respond to increased demand during the pandemic. Elsewhere, departments and parts of the health system are starting to align work more to policy areas and user outcomes in this way.

As we look to the future of digital delivery, it's likely that there will be continued demand for teams to achieve more. We now need to create and maintain new structures around our work, incorporating design approaches that will also enable us to support significant organisation change.

Optimising for the impossible

In chapter 6 we first looked at the idea of reconfiguration, and optimising how we work. We will now revisit this with a specific focus on delivery.

We live in an age where complex build projects are becoming faster and increasingly innovative thanks to design and technology. This is not just innovation in digital products and services, there are examples across the world of mega construction projects being delivered in ways that would have seemed impossible decades ago.

Increasingly, this type of innovation is challenging the cost of building habitable places for people to live and work. This is being driven by new and efficient uses and combinations of materials, manufacturing techniques, shared learning, and reuse.

For over a decade, architecture students at Rural Studio in West Alabama worked on a nearly impossible problem shared around the world: how do you design a home that someone living below the poverty line can afford? In January 2016, after years of building prototypes, the team finished their first pilot project in the real world. Partnering with a commercial developer outside Atlanta in a small local community, they managed to build two one-bedroom houses with materials that cost just $14,000 (about £10,000) each. This was made possible through experimentation and working from first principles, with students totally unpacking what a house is, including the use and cost of its core materials and its construction methods. In doing so they were able to challenge assumptions and rewrite the rules of traditional house building in order to deliver something much more innovative and many times cheaper.[141]

There is a lot we can learn from this. As well as its continued work to develop the construction methods and plans for the house, the studio has also made a commitment to open sourcing the designs to anyone who wants to use them around the world. This is another example of more being possible as long as teams are willing to work in new and innovative ways, with the commitment to experimenting, sharing and building on the work of others.

Just like this affordable house project, when designing and delivering future public services, the opportunity is to optimise how we build. We have already set out the cost benefits and savings of using modern technology solutions, shared code and design systems that provide teams with reusable solutions. But we can continue to push this thinking further.

Expanding how we build

Optimising and expanding how we build is about doing more with the materials and tools at our disposal. In doing so we make delivery a multiplier, because creating efficiencies through how we deliver work means that more can be made possible. It also means that solutions can be created, scaled, and replicated faster.

The key concept is that any type of optimisation creates the flexibility teams and organisations need to focus additional time and effort elsewhere. This might focus on designing, prototyping and testing the non digital parts of a service alongside the development of technology based solutions. It could also be time invested in co-designing and testing solutions with users, as well as directly engaging with communities and places who will be affected by any change to policy and services.

Most of all, this is about helping government tackle its biggest challenges, especially where significant system change is required. Expanding how we build is therefore essential to how the public sector will be able to respond in more radical ways to issues like the climate emergency, as well as current political and policy agendas like Levelling Up.

Modular thinking

Modular thinking is key to optimising delivery. Building on the idea of reconfiguration and breaking things down into their component parts, the emphasis with modular thinking is that individual elements can then be reused, combined as shared capabilities, or reassembled elsewhere.

This has huge potential across the public sector where there are many similar types of service transactions. Taking local government as an example where variations of the same services are found across councils, creating reusable components is more efficient than designing something new every time.

Based on this approach, in 2019 TPXimpact worked with Essex County Council on a project that focused on the reuse of common service patterns. Through a process of discovery, the team identified and mapped around 150 types of interactions residents had with the council. These included a diverse range of goals and needs such as registering a birth, applying for a school place, and reporting a flood.

Within these services, Essex were then able to identify seven core types of patterns including "check something", "book something", and "apply for something". This is a good example of modular thinking, where each pattern has the potential to be designed and tested once, and then reused or reconfigured elsewhere.

In this example, the team found that multiple technology solutions were being used for similar types of user interactions. These instances also required similar types of user flows for people to complete tasks, as well as similar operational dependencies. Consequently, not only was this an opportunity to create more consistent user experiences, it also made it possible to increase the council's use of shared technology components, with the potential for future digital solutions and services to be created more easily and maintained more cheaply. Most importantly, this work has now been open sourced to share service patterns and the data from this project more widely, supporting further conversations about reuse across local government.

Standardising and building in this modular way with patterns that have already been designed and tested elsewhere is something that digital programmes have been good at, including how teams have used and contributed to the NHS and GOV.UK design systems. But these design systems have largely been limited to the User Interface (UI) design of elements that shape the digital parts of services. The opportunity is therefore to also look at the potential to create, test, and scale patterns that include online and offline elements of services, as well as uses of new technology that can help us to meet user needs in more efficient and joined up ways.

This type of design approach within delivery also builds on Government as a Platform, where shared technology solutions are already available and can be easily implemented once organisations have modern cloud based computing approaches in place. However, teams must start by gaining an understanding of all the interactions and capabilities they have from the perspective of citizen needs and the outcomes their organisation supports. It is only from this point that they will be able to optimise everything using more joined up, modular approaches. This is also an example of the type of service organisation thinking we first introduced in chapter 3.

The role of autonomous teams

The most important part of optimising for delivery is through teams. Building from the early work of Government Digital Services (GDS) and GOV.UK, an important principle of digital transformation in the public sector has always been that the unit of delivery is the team.[142] This is the idea in agile delivery that teams must be empowered and trusted – something that we have seen fully justified and acting as the foundation for successful digital delivery responses throughout the pandemic.

How teams use agile to organise their work as part of increasingly large and ambitious programmes of delivery is going to be increasingly important. If we look at large, complex projects in central government or health, work has to be divided into multiple units of delivery, with teams carrying out separate but interdependent work across parts of services. The division and clarity of responsibilities across each team, as well as amongst individuals is crucial to the execution of an overall strategy, enabling everyone to work towards shared goals and outcomes.

In agile delivery, teams must be relative to the size and complexity of the services, or the parts of services they're working on. Organising teams in this way keeps everyone involved in delivery in close proximity to the impact of the work. In practice this means organisations need to keep splitting teams into smaller units of delivery, but in a joined up way that is focused around service outcomes.

This again highlights how in software development and service design, teams need true end to end responsibility for what they design, develop, maintain, support and run. If this then becomes too big or too complex for a team's capacity, the team size can be increased. Ideally however, the focus of the work will be reorganised into smaller parts where there are natural splits, optimising connections between teams, and ensuring teams don't become too big to deliver fast and effectively, or too detached from the real impact of the work they're delivering.[143]

Investment in continuous design and learning

To organise teams capable of making full use of agile principles at scale, it's important to see the design and delivery of services as a continuous process that is never fully done.

As we saw in chapter 4, design as part of delivery needs to be a process of how we put people and their needs at the centre of decision making. Being prepared to question and revisit key assumptions throughout any type of policy or service delivery is key.

This means that there should be no such thing as a service redesign, because this limits any work to a one off set of time boxed activities.

Instead, design as part of delivery has to be continuous, with teams responsible for the outcomes of their work, and how solutions or interventions actually function for people in reality. This level of design maturity is increasingly visible across the public sector where longer term investment has been made in teams and digital programmes focused on service outcomes.

Although discovery is an important initial phase of delivery we also need to embed learning into all the phases of building and improving a service. As Matt Edgar, a Director of Service Transformation at NHSX explains, discovery should be a culture, not just a phase of work. ". . . The distance between discovery and live seems to me wholly misleading. After all, a live, running service affords all sorts of discovery possibilities that wouldn't otherwise exist. . . . In a sufficiently advanced organisation, discovery is a culture, not a phase. Intertwined live service and discovery continually fulfil and refine the purpose of the organisation."[144]

A culture of discovery in delivery means regularly revisiting assumptions and evidence supporting our understanding of user needs. A commitment to continuous improvement through design and delivery means that we might need to stop doing things, as well as commissioning and developing new ideas and technologies. Whatever the answer, more investment is required in user research and the evaluation of solutions and ideas. Organisations must have a clear understanding of how to measure impact, with performance indicators that show how well solutions are working as they are scaled within live environments. Without this focus the impact of digital transformation actually risks making things worse for people.

Done in the right way, and with the support of senior leaders, a longer term commitment to delivering improved outcomes linked to policy will enable organisations to gradually change and evolve how services work and are delivered. This also represents the opportunity to reinvent entire operating models and ways of working enabled by digital solutions and technology.

Moving faster

Although there is value in maintaining many of the changes to delivery approaches taken during the pandemic, we now have the challenge of sustaining the ability to work at pace for longer periods. This includes putting in place the right support and structures for teams as well as ensuring the wellbeing of everyone delivering public sector work.

To fully understand the benefits of delivering services faster, along with continuous design and learning in delivery, we can look more closely at an example – the delivery of the service to provide Covid-19 home testing kits.

At the start of the pandemic, 40% of front line staff in NHS organisations were in isolation with unconfirmed Covid-19 symptoms. In March 2020, TPXimpact worked with NHSX to deliver a new home test kit ordering service, with the goal of ensuring the safety of key workers and enabling those with negative test results to return to work. An initial live service was designed, built and piloted after just seven days in order to meet these urgent requirements.

As part of the live pilot for the service the delivery team asked London Ambulance Service staff to keep a diary, in order to understand their end to end experience and use of the service. Insights from this research, combined with live service data, were then used to make rapid iterations. A dedicated contact centre supporting users with accessibility needs was set up and the service launched fully to all key workers within one month before accepting citizen orders two weeks later.

This example not only highlights an amazing effort by the digital delivery and NHS teams involved, it also shows that with the right focus, it's possible to deliver a brand new service in a matter of days. In this case the team completed initial discovery work in a day, with technical discovery taking place in one further day, and three subsequent days of build. This speed was made possible using existing NHS design patterns, with a modular approach to using reusable code, rapidly prototyping and building key user interactions and journeys for the new service. The results of the home testing kit service speak for themselves, with 67% of key workers helped back to the front line faster, and one million home test kits successfully distributed across the UK within the first three months.[145]

As this case study shows, when we move faster to live, we can find out what works and what doesn't more quickly, discovering new needs which we are then able to meet. When teams have been asked to build solutions like this during Covid-19, this has also meant organisations being more willing to accept minimal viable solutions much earlier. In doing so, key decision makers and stakeholders have also been prepared to accept a little more risk.

We can compare this approach to the more risk averse mindset traditionally seen in the public sector, where teams are forced to move slowly and carefully to avoid any public failure attached to policy and service delivery – whether through ministerial pressure to deliver complete solutions or understandable caution about public spending.

Moving faster without breaking things

It is important to recognise that simply moving fast in the public sector also risks bad outcomes. The technology and innovation mantra of "move fast and break things", can lead to unforeseen circumstances for how services and solutions affect people's lives – especially in the context of everyday needs where the public sector may be their only access to help and support.

As the technologist Terrence Eden (formally of NHSX) explains in his blog post *Things I wish I'd known about NHS Technology*, public services, especially in health, simply can't move fast and break things: "When Facebook updates its UI, that's annoying. When the clinically critical system a doctor uses every day to keep people alive changes the order of its buttons – that's an unacceptable risk. That's why lots of health systems don't receive an update once deployed. Training people costs time and money – and introducing change introduces confusion."[146]

The answer to this is how we support live piloting approaches, recognising the benefits of the learning that comes through delivering something faster. This means piloting solutions in live service situations, but while testing and learning safely through a series of smaller experiments, delivering and managing change incrementally.

This type of approach helps us to ensure high quality and consistent delivery. It recognises that the ability to deliver faster can be beneficial, but also that any level of significant change needs investment and support for front line staff and citizens as part of design in a delivery process.

Piloting is simply about getting real tools, and new uses of technology into people's hands more quickly, enabling more powerful and rapid learning in live service situations. This is what we described in chapter 5 – the importance of shaping new uses of technology with professionals, as well as working more closely with anyone who will need to interact with or use services. The value created from this way of working is feedback – insight and data that teams can respond to as they experiment with different uses of technology, evaluating new ideas and opportunities in real scenarios.

In our Covid-19 home testing kit service, the real learning was the team's ability to get to a live pilot service quickly. This enabled the team to work with live service data and feedback. Understanding the actual experience of Ambulance staff as they ordered kits proved to be the best way to shape the service and add features, making adjustments and expanding research to other roles, user groups and scenarios as the team went along.

Piloting new solutions safely

An important consideration to piloting new solutions is how to do this safely and in a managed way. As with the earlier example of managing risk in the NHS, we have to be able to control what happens if new solutions, technologies or changes to services don't work as intended. So how can we work in this way when our teams and services operate as part of high risk environments?

There are some key considerations for safely piloting services. Firstly, organisations should be prepared to provide additional support via people on the ground who are ready to intervene when something that is being tested breaks or behaves unexpectedly in any way. This could be user researchers shadowing front line staff, or dedicated support workers put in place on a temporary basis. Secondly, and as we have described, teams can test parts of services before gradually expanding the scope of work in a controlled way. This means identifying initial prioritised functionality or capabilities that can be tested in low risk ways. It might involve keeping new solutions detached from more risky parts of existing services or system dependencies to start with.

Working in this way, teams lower the risk and the cost of ideas not working as they are intended to by starting small and scaling slowly through a series of smaller experiments. Again, this is the commitment to transforming services and improving outcomes with continuous design over a longer period of time.

Inverted delivery timelines and light touch assurance processes

What we're not suggesting is the end of Discovery-Alpha-Beta-Live delivery cycles. But instead, being willing to question how quickly ideas and solutions can be deployed to live, inverting traditional delivery timelines. This is how we can prevent new solutions from spending years in slow development cycles, or from being stuck in specification phases of work that don't deliver value to end users quickly enough.

In previous digital delivery models, piloting, or running a live service with a smaller group of users in a controlled situation, was often known as a private beta. The emphasis now is that we need to get to this point much faster as it represents our biggest opportunity for learning.

As these changes have been put into practice during the pandemic, delivery has also been supported by much lighter touch assurance processes – condensed versions of formal service assessments run as Covid-19 peer reviews.[147] While mostly being conducted remotely, these have given teams more flexibility to get solutions to live more quickly, while still ensuring service standards are met.

These changes reflect growing questions around the value of service assessments. Even prior to the pandemic, it was becoming evident that some assurance processes had limited value. While spend control is clearly important, there is a danger that teams simply work towards passing assessment checkpoints, rather than using assurance processes to help them deliver the most value across an entire delivery cycle.

An important point is that if organisations, teams and service areas do move to longer term funding models, then the role of service assessments could change more permanently to light touch, and even more continuous, regular assurance processes. This would allow delivery teams to be more flexible with how they move through different delivery phases of work, with greater support provided by regular peer reviews.

Structures for whole service transformation

After we have moved to pilots and live services faster, the question is then how teams continue to design and deliver solutions, scaling and transforming services in the right ways. A specific challenge is how organisations and teams join up different solutions in a consistent way, as this determines how seamless future user experiences become and to what extent outcomes are improved.

In these situations we need structures for decision making that determine how different technology solutions and the design of different user journeys come together and work in integrated ways.

Part of the solution to this is design principles. In chapter 1 we highlighted when design principles first became part of digital delivery in the UK through the work of the Government Digital Service. These types of guiding principles have since been the basis from which digital transformation teams have made decisions for over a decade, ensuring consistency across solutions developed by hundreds of different teams in multiple organisations.

The GOV.UK design principles, possibly now one of the most famous sets of design principles in the world, state that teams should "Start with user needs", and includes key points such as "Do the hard work to make it simple", and "Make things open: it makes things better". These ideas have successfully guided teams to take user centred approaches, work on shared solutions, and use consistent design patterns to build services that have resulted in more joined up user experiences across the public sector.[148]

Design principles such as these matter because they give everyone a structure for decision making that represents shared values and mission. They indicate what we should do, and also help us determine what not to do. Ultimately, design principles help different teams to make consistent decisions across different parts of delivery and scale joined up services and user experiences in the right ways.

While the GOV.UK design principles are universally applied across the public sector, teams should also be developing their own sets of principles to support shared goals in specific policy or service areas.

Beyond service blueprints

In order to move to live piloting approaches we need to think about service models.

Typically when teams design services they create a service blueprint. Although this is useful for showing the future intended or "to be" state of a service, it's generally a fixed artefact. It doesn't account for what might happen when work comes into contact with real world scenarios.

To continuously design and respond to change we need ways to keep iterating, improving and working with service blueprints in real time. Modelling is a good analogy for transforming whole services, as it's an active process of making ideas, concepts and new ways of working real in an organisation, or as part of the systems teams are working within. This is still service design, but it's about moving all activities more rapidly towards action or learning by doing. Any level of planning should simply be good enough to prototype and pilot viable solutions that we can then work from.

The models we build should be real enough to enable different types of interactions and to evaluate how things work in the real world. They should also help us to work towards an overall vision for how different parts of systems and services start to come together in more joined up ways. Technology, when decoupled and deployed flexibly enough, simply becomes part of the new models we're able to build and scale. This then shapes how services operate through incremental changes, enabling teams to integrate new types of channels and interactions through design and continuous improvement.

Digital delivery that supports system change

Even when delivery teams are asked to build specific digital solutions it's essential they understand the context of their work. This means being willing to examine the systems, connections and relationships that exist in the spaces they are working within.

To create connected, joined up solutions requires more collaborative working and the alignment of priorities and goals. As we have seen, even if teams are delivering single parts of solutions, change requires service design and systems thinking to create improved outcomes through better multi-agency collaboration and data sharing.

In the health sector, this is illustrated through the current intention to achieve more seamless health and care provision via the introduction of Integrated Care Systems (ICSs). These partnerships represent the learning from the pandemic that "people need support which is joined up across local councils, the NHS and voluntary and community organisations".[149] The NHS Long Term Plan confirmed that all parts of England would be served by an ICS from April 2021, removing traditional divisions between hospitals and family doctors, between physical and mental health, and between NHS and council services.

ICSs face the significant challenge of people's increased expectations and the complex range of health and social care needs in society. To deliver more impact, the integration of technology and solutions is needed across these organisations. A fundamental shift is required in how everyone within the health and care system works, with shared purpose and direction, and increasingly collaborative approaches.

Many different delivery teams will contribute to this transformation, with each needing to be aware of how their solutions, and any services they build, will operate as part of a wider system. This means questioning their design decisions with this context in mind, and being willing to consider how they join up work with others more effectively. It includes the ability to apply modular thinking, but without forgetting the need for flexibility around how services may need to adapt to changing local needs and context.

The introduction of Integrated Care Systems demonstrates that outcomes for services like health and care are often far bigger than the remit of any single organisation or delivery team. For this reason the entire public sector needs to be prepared to collaborate more closely in order to effect change within the wider systems we work in.

Most importantly, to achieve this, we need all of our teams to act more like system thinkers. At no point should thinking beyond their particular service or organisation be seen as outside the remit of multi-disciplinary, agile, delivery teams. To shape better outcomes for society, everyone must be committed to understanding how their work fits into a bigger picture of system change.

Leadership for service transformation

A final consideration is the type of leadership needed to support future digital transformation in the public sector. Achieving more requires a new generation of leaders capable of influencing and aligning work across many interdependent parts of our services and systems.

Although it's relatively new, we are already starting to see this model of leadership emerge with roles requiring a design mindset when managing change involving multiple organisations. In areas of the health system like Urgent and Emergency Care, and across major programme areas of The Department for Environment, Food and Rural Affairs (Defra), service leadership roles have been created that are much closer to this remit.

More public sector leaders are also becoming accountable for the vision, direction and quality of whole policy and service areas, meaning that they have responsibility across different interdependencies and for the overall quality of user experience and outcomes being delivered.

This is where leaders can ensure consistency, through the creation of increasingly joined up services and experiences. The opportunity is there for those willing to lead as we start to reimagine and deliver the next generation of public services.

What is made possible

In this chapter we have explored how the public sector needs to use delivery to make more possible.

The key consideration is flexibility. There is no one size fits all approach to how teams should work and how future delivery should be shaped. If anything, it's this flexibility that has been missing as service standards and ways of working have become more aligned and established across the public sector.

Teams now need to be able to pick the right approach for the challenges they face, combining different ways of working where necessary. This includes when to work more closely with communities, as well as considering how to manage change when working as part of complex systems.

The delivery approaches we already have can be adapted, or built upon, giving us space for more experimentation. They can also enable us to work faster and more effectively, piloting live solutions much more quickly and responding in truly agile ways.

In our final chapter we will move on to the challenges of transforming the relationship between the private and public sectors. This includes the need to change procurement and commissioning, as well focusing on our investment in skills, capabilities and social value.

Multiplied Thinking: Key takeaways from chapter 9

- **Reset expectations for future digital delivery.** Question what can be made possible with more flexibility and new sustainable delivery approaches.

- **Optimise how you build.** Evaluate how tools and materials are used and how teams are organised to achieve more.

- **Use modular approaches.** Extend the use of design systems, service patterns and modular thinking that can also shape how technology is implemented and used.

- **Invest in continuous design and learning.** Organise and fund teams and priorities around service and policy areas with a mindset of continuous discovery.

- **Move faster with a live piloting approach.** Recognise the benefits of delivering live services faster, inverting traditional digital delivery models, while also testing and learning safely.

- **Focus on whole service transformation.** Guide decision making with design principles, and use service models as an approach to live service delivery while working towards system change.

10 Transforming commissioning, skills, and social value

"Price is what you pay. Value is what you get."

– Warren Buffett[150]

In part 2 of the book we have focused on the use of design, technology, data, and delivery to create and deliver more value – considering how to increase the return on investment in digital transformation and services.

In this final chapter we will look at how external suppliers can work more effectively with the public sector. This is an important question for us at TPXimpact as we believe the public sector should demand more value from its commercial arrangements, and that it's time to reset expectations around how work is delivered, and the types of outcomes and impact this leads to.

There is also a pressing need to build sustainable capability in the digital workforce, both by bringing in external support and through investment in upskilling in house teams, taking collective responsibility to address skills gaps. Beyond the delivery of services themselves, there is now increased focus on how publicly funded work should create wider benefits for society.

It is social value – the difference the public sector's work makes to people, communities and planet – that will determine the impact of future digital transformation and change. If we truly believe in creating meaningful outcomes for society, then we have to help communities, organisations and businesses in their eventual recovery from Covid-19, while also tackling inequality, and responding to future challenges including the climate emergency.

Transforming public sector procurement and commissioning

The starting point for understanding how the public sector realises value through its commercial arrangements is found in its procurement practices. It's important to consider how we might transform the role of suppliers in this context, as well as holding government to account where reform is already underway, and increasing ambition for what can be made possible.

Rather than just focus on procurement – which, by definition, is more the act of purchasing – it is in the broader scope of commissioning where there is the opportunity to apply the type of thinking explored throughout this book. When considering how the public sector finds and works with suppliers, this is everything from identifying a need, to buying consultancy services, and then managing the delivery of work, as well as measuring its impact.

The Digital Marketplace

To understand the progress that has already been made in transforming public sector procurement and commissioning, we can look briefly at the history of the Digital Marketplace.

Now run by the Crown Commercial Service (CCS), the Digital Marketplace was, until 2019, managed and overseen by the Government Digital Service (GDS). Its purpose is to source technology or people for digital projects within the public sector. When first created, the intent was that it would reduce reliance on the same, large suppliers who had dominated the market for decades and prevent repeats of IT project failures – just like the The British Army Jobs example we shared in chapter 6. It was also designed to create a more diverse supplier market, making opportunities available to businesses across the UK.

While organisations still use a number of other commercial frameworks, the Digital Marketplace has dramatically changed the procurement landscape over the past decade. It has created exactly the sort of competitive contract supplier market that it was designed to, with a marketplace of smaller, more diverse businesses bidding for public sector work. However, there are still significant challenges with how organisations are able to get the most value from the commercial arrangements they use to support digital transformation work.

The reality today is that procurement is still relatively slow and complicated for both buyers and suppliers to navigate.

Although the Digital Marketplace has opened up a more diverse supplier market, it hasn't led to a move away from process driven and document heavy tender requirements. Formulaic processes, with steps mapped out in advance, are designed to protect both buyers and suppliers from legal challenge, and to ensure fairness and transparency in how contracts are awarded. Yet these processes allow for little flexibility. They also don't guarantee delivery of work that will create the most possible value – both value for money, and how value can be measured through the impact of work.

Faced with these frustrations, there are growing numbers of advocates for agile procurement practices using the same types of agile processes, tools, skills and ceremonies that we might expect to use in delivery.

This is also reflected in reform underway at the centre of government, with a green paper, *Transforming Public Procurement*, published in December 2020.[151] This sets out the intention to ensure that more value is released from public spending. To summarise, the recommendations include:

- making processes more compatible with modern, agile ways of developing and using digital technology
- increasing transparency with digitally published expenditure to allow all interested parties to see costs and benefits, creating an open, accountable and more trustworthy system
- increasing local collaboration, developing more services around the knowledge and expertise of social enterprises and charities, who have a vested interest in providing services that work at the ground level with communities
- taking a more strategic view, with a longer term outlook on issues that encompass needs as well as outcomes (not just viewing procurement as a way to deliver a single product or service)
- moving the award process away from the most economically advantageous tender (the cheapest) to the most advantageous tender (the one with potential to deliver the most value)

The green paper and subsequent reform work since December 2020 represents good intentions, but the public sector should be more ambitious and go even further.

Increasing the value of public spending on digital transformation

Along with a shared ambition for change, it's the quality and strength of the relationships between the public and private sectors, and the way we incorporate feedback and learning to work more collaboratively, that has the potential to multiply the impact of our work together in the future.

We now need public institutions willing to engage with the market, who want to listen and learn, as well as being open to new ideas and innovation. In turn, the public sector needs suppliers that will listen to feedback, adjusting their ways of working to respond to the changing needs of the sector.

Earlier and extended engagement

One key area where the public and private sectors can collaborate more closely is in how opportunities are shaped as they come to market.

The first part of any commissioning process is identifying and agreeing requirements. This means making assumptions explicit about the outcomes and services needed, and how they're likely to be delivered. In the public sector, a key part of shaping requirements for a solution is how organisations understand user needs. It should be the case that user needs shape requirements, which then inform decisions about how work is delivered.

The introduction of service standards over the past decade means that most advertised opportunities brought to the external supplier market now include a set of user needs that has been identified. However, this also introduces the immediate risk that these needs have been based on assumptions, rather than informed by evidence and the effective use of research.

In order to deliver solutions that will create the most value, suppliers could play more of an active role in shaping requirements and challenging assumptions, with this work forming part of commissioning. This includes offering support for workshops, conducting early exploratory research, and helping to consolidate previous work in order to provide the strongest possible starting point for teams. This is especially important where there has been a significant gap in time between previous research or engagement activities taking place and new delivery work being commissioned. For this purpose, organisations could prioritise shorter periods of discovery work – days or weeks, rather than months.

This is also the opportunity to make citizen engagement a part of commissioning processes – either through a formal engagement process, or through the way work and requirements are created using local democratic processes like citizens' assemblies.

Ensuring value is demonstrated faster

Another key area where the public and private sectors need to collaborate in new ways is ensuring that all work demonstrates value faster. This can be measured by how quickly people are able to experience improved outcomes as the result of investment in digital transformation, policy and services.

As we have already highlighted, delivering real value for people faster can mean real outcomes being delivered in weeks, not months or years. In chapter 6, we even set out why it's important to ensure that suppliers are incentivised to demonstrate value quickly, or face handing over the work to others. This is an example of how commissioning processes will also require new types of contract management – the monitoring processes after contracts are awarded that ensure value is being delivered in the right ways.

A good example that demonstrates the need to demonstrate value faster is the ongoing work to transform breast screening in the NHS, shared with us by Noel Gordon, former chair of NHS Digital and non executive director of NHS England.

Historically, screening systems and patient pathways have been incredibly disjointed, and among NHS leaders there's a shared feeling, supported by evidence, that better health outcomes could and should be enabled by technology and innovation – as we first explored in chapter 7.

Technology can support radiologists in the early detection of cancer. In the UK, every woman's screening mammogram is read by two radiologists, who decide independently whether she needs to be recalled for further examination. This "double reading screening" is considered the medical gold standard yet it can be difficult to achieve due to a global shortage of radiologists. In an example of how technology can support clinical outcomes, Artificial Intelligence (AI) can replace the second reader and work alongside a human counterpart, creating additional capacity, as well as benefiting radiologists by improving the accuracy of each diagnosis.[152]

Technology clearly offers significant opportunities, but in this story we also find a huge problem with delivery.

The intention in these situations is to move cautiously. This means ensuring technologies are carefully evaluated, introduced ethically, and without causing harm or adversely impacting patients. However, in an effort to future proof investment in improving the service, and to manage the risk of implementing such technologies, the NHS found itself stalled in a specification stage. Rather than deliver something faster that could be built on in the future, they got caught up in explaining everything in detail upfront. As a consequence, it will take much longer for the system to gain the additional capacity it needs, and for women to benefit from improved clinical outcomes. In the meantime, since this use of technology is not yet able to support radiologists, women are not being called back for further examinations as quickly as they could be.

When we look back at the commissioning models that enable this kind of situation, the pattern that we see again and again is starting requirements becoming so broad and comprehensive that they become undeliverable. When a digital transformation initiative begins with this type of over specification, it quickly becomes a waste of time and money, with costs disproportionately spent on managing requirements and the complexity of the entire project scope. This goes against everything we have explored so far when our goal should be to deliver improved outcomes for people, faster.

So how could the transformation of breast screening services have worked instead? A viable piloting approach for this project could have been developed in weeks or, at the very least, months. It would have represented a minimal, viable solution that, to start with, could have been tested in a single hospital, or with a single team of radiologists. Any new use of technology could then have been closely monitored and evaluated as part of existing clinical practices and ways of working, with additional checks in place and user researchers on the ground to observe how radiologists are working with the new system.

There are obviously many factors to consider when ensuring that people benefit from a new use of technology, and that there are no unintended consequences from experimenting in this way. But starting small, and testing solutions in a live service environment would have allowed the NHS to evaluate this use of AI more quickly. From here, they would have been able to gradually scale this within a single hospital, then in an NHS Trust and group of hospitals, before moving regionally, and eventually delivering a shared national solution at scale.

This way of working also creates the space for front line staff to play a crucial role in shaping new uses of technology. In this instance, more detailed engagement with NHS staff could also have taken place during early pilots in order to build relevant evaluation and performance frameworks – enabling the longer term monitoring of any continued investment at scale in the AI technology.

While contractually there is still a need to limit funding, we have to be prepared to look for smaller ways to experiment – learning through incremental delivery and looking to gradual funding that supports new ideas as value is demonstrated.

Sharing, extending, and building on what works

Not only is working in the open important in this type of example, so is sharing knowledge, solutions and platforms – with organisations building on the work of others, and becoming active collaborators in shared solutions that can benefit everyone within a wider system.

As well as bringing an important outside perspective to public sector work, suppliers should also be sharing what they've learned. This includes knowledge gained from any work delivered inside the public sector and beyond – helping to grow and sustain knowledge networks and connections between different organisations.

The important opportunity is inherited knowledge from previous contracts. If a supplier is commissioned to work in an area like health or housing, then buyers should benefit from all of their previous experience of working within these systems and policy areas. This should act like a shortcut, bringing starting hypotheses to the table about what has worked elsewhere, and why. There should be no question of the free and unrestricted access to this knowledge – anything that can be reused should be reused to ensure the strongest possible starting point for new work.

This doesn't only have to include individual projects or work within specific contracts. Suppliers should also play an active role in creating and sustaining wider networks and the sharing of ideas, helping organisations collaborate and build on work started elsewhere.

This type of connection-building opens up opportunities for wider participation in the transformation of services, with stronger links into knowledge held by other partners including the voluntary and community sector. For example, through years of experience in digital transformation, TPXimpact has many established networks with local government and its partners. The ability to use these links when working with national policy or central agencies is important as it creates opportunities for community participation and hyper-local approaches. In health, this might be the links between social care, the role of a council and the way organisations work with national policy while transforming local services with a community. This joined up way of working becomes especially important once we see how local links with communities can shape relationships and solve problems in a more targeted way.

If we want to be radical about reshaping commissioning to create more value, then potential partners should be required to demonstrate the depth and strength of their networks, their knowledge within different sectors, and the extent to which they can make practical use of this – for example, their ability to apply innovation through technology in a particular domain they already have experience in. Organisations can then start to evaluate this type of value more formally as part of procurement.

While the complexity and scale of different policy areas means that it's almost impossible to completely eliminate the repetition of work in different places, individual parts of the public sector can make better use of existing data, research and technology solutions developed elsewhere by creating better knowledge networks. All of this represents better value for money, while also providing the potential for faster delivery of live solutions.

Investment in skills and capability

Most public sector organisations are now actively investing in their own digital skills and communities of practice, supported by the development of professional specialist government frameworks like DDaT (Digital, Data and Technology).[153] Some organisations have been building teams in areas like design, data science and engineering for more than 5-10 years now, with digital capabilities central to their ability to deliver new types of products, services and solutions and to work in new ways.

External suppliers also have an important role to play. Increasingly, organisations are looking to commercial routes to access the digital skills and experience they need. For many, this is because recruitment is a significant challenge, especially with limits around salaries and benefits. But it's also a reflection on the need for flexibility as new and existing programmes scale up to deliver policy and change initiatives.

The emphasis of many programmes is therefore to fill delivery gaps with specific digital roles such as User Researchers, Business Analysts, and Software Developers, working alongside other suppliers, or as part of blended teams with in house employees. TPXimpact are currently user research, design, product delivery, and product management partners with parts of government including the Department for Education and HM Land Registry, supporting teams across these organisations to grow their skills and maturity across programmes of work.

This type of partnership has seen the emergence of multi-supplier models with several private sector agencies working together on a single programme of work, each providing different specialist roles. However, in house teams don't always get as much value as they could from suppliers when they work in this way. Reasons for this include not having a single supplier to hold to account for the delivery of service outcomes, as well as not seeing the value of the collective experience and ways of working that a complete team from a single supplier can provide.

This approach also creates significant overhead for teams having to manage multiple supplier and commercial arrangements, and it can leave individuals feeling exposed if placed into programmes on their own, and without familiar team structures or ways of working. All of this points to the need to think carefully about the blend of roles, and approach to involving multiple suppliers in a single delivery programme.

Investing in a future public sector workforce

External suppliers are important to the public sector because they bring new perspectives, introducing teams and organisations to new ideas and innovative ways of working. This is an important aspect of any capability support work. Suppliers, and the specialists they provide, must upskill the people and teams they work with. This should be through growing communities of practice, as well as helping teams on a more individual basis with appropriate challenge and support.

To create more value from public spending in this way, all suppliers should be transparently allocating a percentage of overall contract costs towards training and upskilling the next generation of public servants. The goal here is to increase in house skills and the number of specialists working inside the public sector, investing in a digitally skilled future workforce.

This will also require the public sector to be willing to receive and work with junior talent, perhaps in paired work with more experienced digital specialists. Creating a future workforce requires apprentices and trainees to get real delivery experience. The private and public sectors therefore need to work together to provide positive environments and learning opportunities for the next generation.

In taking this approach we will start to ease the digital, data, and technology skills shortages that affect both the public and private sectors. As we have already explored, the ability to increase digital skill sets will not only help organisations to deliver future technology solutions, but will also be essential to reshaping how teams are able to think and act. This is essential to severing any total future reliance on external suppliers and managing the costs of delivery more effectively.

Extending social value

Following the December 2020 Transforming Public procurement green paper, the Cabinet Office issued further guidance setting out how public spending should be supporting a range of other outcomes including job creation and boosts for skills training, helping small businesses grow, and supporting the UK's Covid-19 pandemic recovery.

Aimed at the NHS, as well as central and local government, this represents an ambition to deliver more value from the £290 billion a year that is currently spent in the public sector. Legislation was subsequently passed in January 2021, that means anyone now bidding for work has to demonstrate how they will deliver additional social value as part of contracts.

With the right ambition and focus, social value should lead to better outcomes for people and the places they live. It is aimed at ensuring public spending tackles inequality, and supports new businesses, jobs and skills. In addition, the social value delivered through future commercial contracts is intended to help society fight climate change, and improve wider social outcomes such as health. For the public sector, this should also provide new ways of managing demand for support, while ensuring a more joined up, consistent approach to how different services deliver the best possible outcomes.[154]

All of this makes social value a multiplier. Investment in both national and local services should help smaller businesses to grow, as well as strengthening links into voluntary and community organisations. This is also how the public sector can create and sustain opportunities for people across the country as part of any levelling up agenda.

There is still a long way to go for public institutions to make social value an effective part of their commercial contracts. However, what we can do is look more closely at key areas where the way work is commissioned and delivered should now be creating wider benefits for society.

Tackling workforce inequality

We have already talked about the value of developing future digital skills within the workforce. An increased emphasis on social value should focus organisations on building a more diverse and inclusive workforce that reflects their communities. This includes better representation across ethnicity, gender, disability, sexuality, religion and the age demographics of teams.

For this to happen, the private sector should be actively investing in positively shaping its own workforces and tackling inequality in the workplace. When demonstrating social value as part of contracts, it's essential that all suppliers evidence their own investment in creating and sustaining diverse and inclusive teams, as well as being able to show the representation of people across all levels of leadership including company boards and management teams.

As we help to build the future models of our public institutions, suppliers must also create inclusive environments throughout their employee experiences. Genuine inclusivity in the workplace requires consistent commitment, from recruitment to exit interviews, with transparent reporting processes, funded employee resource groups, and communities of practice capable of promoting and offering peer support for underrepresented groups.

Creating and extending opportunities

An important part of social value is how public spending benefits people through the creation of new jobs and opportunities. This is the opportunity to provide learning and upskilling opportunities to people inside our public institutions, and to those working and volunteering in the communities we work with when delivering services.

Upskilling can take many forms depending on the situation. It could be offering people the opportunity to learn to code, or increasing awareness about specific digital disciplines and roles. Whatever options they choose, suppliers should be committing to creating and promoting opportunities for people to learn new skills as part of every piece of work that's commissioned. This must happen in a strategic way, with the establishment of paid apprenticeship programmes and fast track schemes, for example, being integrated with real career pathways.

An important question is who will really benefit from the creation of new opportunities, jobs and training. This is especially the case when we consider regional economic investment and job creation. Given the success of hybrid and more flexible working we can now open up opportunities that might not have been accessible to many people before the pandemic. It is now possible to build teams across the whole country, without having to restrict opportunities to those able to commute into city centre hubs and shared office spaces.

As the government green paper explains, the benefits of public spending should also unleash opportunities for small businesses, charities and social enterprises. The use of local supply chains, and the ability for larger suppliers to partner with new, smaller and more local businesses is also important in creating regional growth. As we have seen in examples like the UK vaccination programme, the role of local connections, if funded and supported properly, is vital to the reach and effectiveness of services. In areas such as health, and young people's services, we need local knowledge, engagement and trust to ensure that services improve outcomes and reach everyone in the right ways.

Responding to the climate emergency

As we face the climate emergency, the next major crisis of our time, we must consider the environmental implications of the public sector's work, including its supply chains. In line with the government's Carbon Reduction Plan, suppliers must now demonstrate the steps they're taking to reduce their own effect on the environment as part of commercial public sector contracts.[155] TPXimpact's Carbon Reduction Plan confirms our commitment to achieving net zero by 2050. This means that we're committed to reducing our scope 1 and 2 emissions to zero before 2027. From the scope 3 categories, we will reduce emissions by at least 50% by 2030 and by 90% before 2050.[156]

Considerations should also include how any office space is leased and maintained as well as how work is organised to limit the environmental impact of how people travel and co-locate. However, suppliers can, and should go further than this.

Digital technology also requires electricity generation, which within current energy supply chains often involves the burning of fossil fuels. Suppliers delivering technology based solutions should therefore now be looking to achieve near real time carbon reporting as part of monitoring their environmental impact. This will mean working with cloud vendors to calculate the carbon footprint of technology solutions and hosting, reporting this to clients transparently and planning for offset. Amazon, Google and Microsoft are already making significant progress in providing tools to do this, putting the onus on government and industry to act.[157]

Good carbon practices must now be aligned with every modern organisation's design and software development practices. Technology teams should be using serverless technologies, as well as working to reduce unnecessary processing power. Where we have control, this means using products and platforms that are hosted in data centres run from renewable energy sources. The reuse of solutions and service components is also an environmental consideration. To limit carbon emissions, teams should make lightweight, accessible, efficient design choices as part of managing the environmental effects of the solutions they create. The use of design systems, frameworks, and shared platforms all enables teams to optimise the building and deployment of solutions.

Most importantly, facing daunting climate statistics, we will need to rapidly move beyond reducing carbon emissions. Suppliers now have an important role to play in helping the public sector to be bold in how it responds to the climate emergency. Any new vision, and our ability to create a different type of story for the future, will require us to collectively design regenerative places that improve the lives of local people, while also balancing the needs of the planet.

Creating joined up services and improved outcomes

The extension of social value is dependent on a more joined up, collaborative public sector that will reduce waste in our systems. This recognises the need for new commercial work to build stronger links into existing solutions, and become more capable of building on the work of others. There is also the need to manage demand for services and support using joined up approaches that make the best use of digital transformation and technology to extend the reach and flexibility of solutions.

As we invest more in the whole transformation of services, suppliers must understand that a truly joined up approach to how organisations work together and share initiatives is needed. Service areas and organisations have to collaborate effectively if we're going to see improvements to health and wellbeing in society, with opportunities for all through education, and flexible support when people need it throughout their lives.

The sum of our parts

The future of our work together needs to be more than just the sum of our parts. In this final chapter, we have looked at how the public sector needs a competitive marketplace that is able to draw from the skills, knowledge, and networks of a range of businesses and social enterprises.

Looking at how suppliers can deliver more value, we have seen that procurement and commissioning is already changing, but there is the potential to do more with how we challenge and shape opportunities and build on the work of others.

We have focused on extending social value to ensure that public spending benefits local places and economies, creating opportunities and tackling inequality. We have also looked specifically at the importance of building digital skills as part of a new public sector workforce, recognising that there is a need to create sustainable in house capabilities to support long term delivery.

Underpinning all of this is an opportunity to create genuine partnerships that will make sure we're prepared to collectively respond to future challenges. It is how we collaborate and the relationships we build that become multipliers. There will also be better assurances that public money is being spent wisely on transforming services that reach and benefit all of society in fairer and more sustainable ways.

Multiplied Thinking: Key takeaways from chapter 10

- **Transforming the relationship between the public and private sector.** Incorporate transparent feedback and learning to work more collaboratively, increasing expectations for the value that can be created through procurement and commissioning.

- **Support earlier and extended engagement.** Work more closely with suppliers to challenge starting assumptions and to better understand user needs when shaping requirements. Consider how to incorporate citizen engagement in the early stages of commissioning.

- **Ensure value is demonstrated faster.** Limit contract value and sizes where necessary to ensure people benefit from investment in technology and change more quickly.

- **Share, extend and build on what works.** Work with suppliers to realise the full benefits of working in the open, building on the work of others and making the best use of existing knowledge and experience.

- **Invest in future skills and capability.** Expect suppliers to invest in skills development and capability building as part of contracts. Ensure that in house teams can respond in the right way to future challenges and that public institutions continue to benefit from new and outside perspectives.

- **Extend the social value of work.** Work with suppliers to create wider societal benefits for people and communities through any investment in digital transformation, extending the reach and impact of work in society.

Multiplied

To reinforce what we said at the start of the book, now is the time to be bold and to reset our expectations for what is possible. Digital transformation can and should deliver more impact for the public sector, helping us to meet future challenges and create a new generation of public services and support.

We need to be ambitious. We have an opportunity to rebuild and reimagine society, including how we reshape our public institutions as they continue to respond to change.

Thanks to the talented people and teams we are privileged to work with every single day, the public sector, as well as the voluntary and community sector, are amazing places to work. You just have to look at the people working alongside you to know there is incredible potential in what might now be possible. We all want to make a positive difference and improve outcomes, with the impact of our work reaching everyone in communities across the country.

We have the individual and collective responsibility to build these positive futures. Doing this means learning to recognise the multipliers in our work – from people, teams, participation and inclusion, to how we work with design, technology and data in delivery. Most importantly, it is how we work with each other – helping our organisations to collaborate more closely, share solutions and achieve more together.

We all have to be prepared to start somewhere. To work differently, and to apply new thinking and ways of responding to change. It's okay to start small, but we must also think big.

Change is inevitable, and everything is possible, so let's make a start.

References

Chapter 1

1 Erling Kagge, *"Walking: One step at a time"* (Quote by the late Norwegian Philosopher Arne Naess), Penguin, March 2020

2 Adapted from Public Digital, *"Definition of Digital"*, https://public.digital/definition-of-digital

3 GDS, *"Government Digital Service: Our strategy for 2021-2024"*, May 2021 https://gds.blog.gov.uk/2021/05/20/government-digital-service-our-strategy-for-2021-2024/

4 NHS, *"Long Term plan"*, January 2019 https://www.longtermplan.nhs.uk/

5 Civil Service World, *"NHS Digital and NHSX to be merged into NHS England"*, November 2021 *https://www.civilserviceworld.com/professions/article/nhs-digital-and-nhsx-to-be-merged-into-nhs-england-25977*

6 LocalGov Camp https://localgov.digital/events/localgovcamp

7 UK Government, *"DDaT profession"* https://www.gov.uk/government/organisations/digital-data-and-technology-profession

8 GDS, *"GDS Academy turns 5 and celebrates training 10,000 students"*, February 2019 https://gds.blog.gov.uk/2019/02/20/gds-academy-turns-5-and-celebrates-training-10000-students/

9 Simon Parker, *"Nothing can change"*, March 2020 https://medium.com/@SimonFParker/nothing-can-change-f20bd6dbc60d

10 DfE Digital, *"DfE's digital and technology strategy"*, April 2021 https://dfedigital.blog.gov.uk/2021/04/21/strategy/

Chapter 2

11 Hillary Cottam, *"Radical Help: How we can remake the relationships between us and revolutionise the welfare state"*, Virago, June 2018

12 BBC, *"Blackburn launches a coronavirus tracing service to contact people NHS Test and Trace fails to find"*, August 2020 https://www.bbc.co.uk/news/uk-england-lancashire-53648362

13 BBC, *"Several councils did not receive up-to-date Covid data for almost three weeks, the BBC learns"*, May 2021 https://www.bbc.co.uk/news/uk-politics-57186059

14 BBC, *"Newcastle vaccine bus parks up at hard-to-reach communities"*, March 2021 https://www.bbc.co.uk/news/av/uk-england-tyne-56325136

15 Andy Burnham, *"Our Over-Centralised Westminster System Has Too Long Prioritised Investment Inside The M25 - That May Be About To Change"*, March 2018 https://www.huffingtonpost.co.uk/entry/convention-of-the-north_uk_5b8b9a2de4b0511db3d96d5c

16 UK Government, *"New levelling up and community investments"*, March 2021 https://www.gov.uk/government/collections/new-levelling-up-and-community-investments

17 TPXimpact, *"Blackpool Climate Assembly"* https://www.tpximpact.com/our-work/blackpool-climate-assembly

18 UK Government, *"Build back better: Our plan for growth"*, March 2021 https://www.gov.uk/government/publications/build-back-better-our-plan-for-growth

19 Craig Morbay, *"A community voice in Blackpool"*, April 2021 https://www.tpximpact.com/insights/blackpool-community-voice

20 Wigan Council, *"The Deal Brochure"* https://www.wigan.gov.uk/Docs/PDF/Council/The-Deal/The-Deal-Brochure.pdf

21 Wigan Council, *"The Deal"* https://www.wigan.gov.uk/Council/The-Deal

22 Steve Butterworth, *"We must all step up to support our communities"*, June 2020 https://www.localgov.co.uk/We-must-all-step-up-to-support-our-communities-/50648

23 Harpenden Cares https://harpendencares.org/about

24 Leeds City Council, *"Using neighbourhood networks to connect communities"*, October 2021 https://www.local.gov.uk/case-studies/leeds-city-council-using-neighbourhood-networks-connect-communities

25 Towns Fund https://www.gov.uk/government/collections/towns-fund

26 NASA Earth Observatory, *"Global temperatures"*, https://earthobservatory.nasa.gov/world-of-change/global-temperatures

27 COP21, *"COP26 keeps 1.5C alive and finalises Paris Agreement"*, November 2021 https://ukcop26.org/cop26-keeps-1-5c-alive-and-finalises-paris-agreement/

28 ICC, *"Summary for Policymakers of IPCC Special Report on Global Warming of 1.5°C approved by governments"*, October 2018 https://www.ipcc.ch/2018/10/08/summary-for-policymakers-of-ipcc-special-report-on-global-warming-of-1-5c-approved-by-governments/

29 Royal Borough of Greenwich, "Plans to change streets to ensure safe transport for all", June 2020 https://www.royalgreenwich.gov.uk/news/article/1622/plans_to_change_streets_to_ensure_safe_transport_for_all_post-lockdown

Chapter 3

30 Umair Haque, *"(How to Build) The Organizations of the Future"*, April 2018 https://eand.co/how-to-build-the-organizations-of-the-future-f2c6aefd33b6

31 UK Government, *"Agile and government services: an introduction"* https://www.gov.uk/service-manual/agile-delivery/agile-government-services-introduction

32 IFS, *"5.3 million people waiting for NHS treatment in May 2021, up from 4.4 million in February 2020"*, August 2021 https://ifs.org.uk/publications/15557

33 Milton Freeman quote from: David Sax, *" The Revenge of Analog: Real Things and Why They Matter"*, PublicAffairs, Reprint edition, October 2017

34 Chris Naylor quote from: *"Policy Outlook for 2022 and Beyond"*, Solace Summit, October 2021

35 Nassim Nicholas Taleb, *"Surgeons Should Not Look Like Surgeons"*, February 2017 https://medium.com/incerto/surgeons-should-notlook-like-surgeons-23b0e2cf6d52

36 HBR, *"When CEOs talk strategy is anyone listening?"*, June 2013 https://hbr.org/2013/06/when-ceos-talk-strategy-is-anyone-listening

37 Based on vision as a useful end state description – taken from: Rutger Bregman, *"Utopia for Realists"*, De Correspondent, November 2016

38 Digital Salford https://www.digitalsalford.com/about-salford/

39 Stephen Fry, *"Q&A: The success of Salford's Digital You project"*, November 2018 https://www.govtechleaders.com/2018/11/09/qa-the-success-of-salfords-digital-you-project/

40 Dr Pippa Grange, *"Fear Less: How to Win at Life Without Losing Yourself"*, Vermilion, July 2020

41 Rob Hopkins, *"From What Is to What If: Unleashing the power of imagination to create the future we want"*, Chelsea Green Publishing, October 2019

42 Ben Holliday, *"A House without windows"*, September 2019 https://www.hollidazed.co.uk/2019/09/13/a-house-without-windows/

43 Matt Jukes, *"Lessons from the public service response to Covid-19"*, September 2021 https://www.tpximpact.com/insights/lessons-from-the-public-service-response-to-covid-19

44 Royal Borough of Greenwich, *"We've published our first digital strategy at the Royal Borough of Greenwich"*, November 2020 https://www.royalgreenwich.gov.uk/blog/digital/post/103/we%E2%80%99ve-published-our-first-digital-strategy-at-the-royal-borough-of-greenwich

45 The idea of Service Organisations is based upon the work of Kate Tarling https://katetarling.com/

46 DfE Digital, *"Introducing a Head of Digital role to DfE"*, May 2021 https://dfedigital.blog.gov.uk/2021/05/28/head-of-digital/

47 Parkinson's UK, *"Our vision, mission and values"* https://www.parkinsons.org.uk/about-us/our-vision-mission-and-values

48 Parkinson's UK Service Transformation, *"The Challenge Ahead"*, May 2019 https://parkinsonsukst.medium.com/the-challenge-ahead-443e9300f35c

49 Parkingson's UK, *"Parkinson's Connect: our new support service"*, February 2020 https://www.parkinsons.org.uk/news/parkinsons-connect-our-new-support-service

50 Parkinson's UK, *"Parkinson's Connect: how we're evolving Parkinson's support"*, October 2021 https://www.parkinsons.org.uk/news/parkinsons-connect-how-were-evolving-parkinsons-support

Chapter 4

51 Jay-Z, *Empire State Of Mind* song lyrics

52 IDEO, Design Thinking https://designthinking.ideo.com/history

53 Design Council, *"Double Diamond after 15 years"*, September 2019 https://www.designcouncil.org.uk/news-opinion/double-diamond-15-years

54 Adapted from Lily Dart, Twitter thread https://twitter.com/lily_dart/status/1446401718049202185

55 GDS, *"Have you had your recommended dose of research?"*, June 2014 https://userresearch.blog.gov.uk/2014/08/06/have-you-had-your-recommended-dose-of-research/

56 Ian Leslie, *"Conflicted: Why Arguments Are Tearing Us Apart and How They Can Bring Us Together"*, Faber & Faber, February 2021

57 Ben Holliday, Tweet, *"Creating a digital delivery culture"*, October 2015 https://twitter.com/benholliday/status/657085783250227200

58 Ben Holliday, *"Simple models"*, May 2019 https://www.hollidazed.co.uk/2019/05/08/simple-models/

59 Vitsoe Design Dieter Rams, *"Ten principles for good design"*, https://www.vitsoe. com/gb/about/good-design

60 GDS, *"Government Design Principles"* https://www.gov.uk/guidance/government-design-principles#do-the-hard-work-to-make-it-simple

61 GDS, *"Simpler Carer's Allowance digital service now live"*, November 2014 https:// gds.blog.gov.uk/2014/11/28/simpler-carers-allowance-digital-service-now-live/

62 Design Questioning originally based on an idea presented by Liz Jackson: New Adventures Conference, *"Productivity recreates disability"*, January 2020 https:// www.youtube.com/watch?v=O5abEgBQ3ZM

63 Ben Holliday, *"Asking the right questions to frame the problem"*, July 2015 https:// www.hollidazed.co.uk/2015/07/28/frame-the-problem/

64 The Guardian, *"Economics is a failing discipline doing great harm – so let's rethink it"*, August 2019 https://www.theguardian.com/commentisfree/2019/aug/03/economics-global-economy-climate-crisis

65 Sky News, *"Coronavirus: The inside story of how government failed to develop a contact-tracing app"*, July 2020 https://news.sky.com/story/coronavirus-the-inside-story-of-how-government-failed-to-develop-a-contact-tracing-app-12031282

66 Anthony King, Ivor Crewe, *"The Blunders of Our Governments"*, Oneworld Publications, September 2013

67 Additional design questioning themes explored in talk by Ben Holliday, *"UX Bristol 2021: Asking Design Questions"*, July 2021 https://www.youtube.com/watch?v=wX1YFn8ujgo

68 Sky News, Dr Michael J Ryan WHO press conference, March 2020 https:// twitter.com/skynews/status/1238504143104421888

69 CNN, February 2002 https://www.youtube.com/watch?v=REWeBzGuzCc

70 Ben Holliday, *"Ambiguity and design"*, December 2018 https://www.hollidazed. co.uk/2018/12/01/ambiguity-and-design/

71 Environment, Food and Rural Affairs Committee, July 2021 https://www. parliamentlive.tv/Event/Index/c7402fc6-93b8-4a34-92ab-3d818699c99d

72 Ben Holliday, *"Everything is hypothesis driven design"*, July 2015 https://www. hollidazed.co.uk/2015/07/16/everything-is-hypothesis-driven-design/

73 Ben Holliday, *"Collective, small, actions as culture"*, August 2017 https://www. hollidazed.co.uk/2017/08/28/collective-small-actions-as-culture/

Chapter 5

74   Madeleine Albright, former US Secretary of State (quote starts at 21:16), *"David M. Rubenstein Lecture"*, February 2019 https://www.youtube.com/watch?v=G9dmPGiC2vQ&t=2s

75   Matt Jukes, *"Lessons from the public service response to covid-19"*, September 2021 https://www.tpximpact.com/insights/lessons-from-the-public-service-response-to-covid-19

76   Excerpt from the description of principle number 12: NHS, *"NHS Service Manual"* https://service-manual.nhs.uk/service-standard

77   UK Government, *"Service Manual: Making Source Code Open and Reusable"* https://www.gov.uk/service-manual/technology/making-source-code-open-and-reusable

78   Essex County Council, *"It's just a website, we aren't going to the moon"*, June 2020 https://servicetransformation.blog.essex.gov.uk/2020/06/10/its-just-a-website-we-arent-going-to-the-moon

79   Sarah Finch, *"3 minutes on . . . No code"*, October 2021 https://www.tpximpact.com/insights/3-minutes-on-no-code

80   MoJ Digital & Technology, *"Rapidly delivering an online form using MoJ Form Builder"*, July 2020 https://mojdigital.blog.gov.uk/2020/07/22/rapidly-delivering-an-online-form-using-moj-form-builder/

81   GDS, *"Government as a Platform the next phases of digital transformation"*, March 2015 https://gds.blog.gov.uk/2015/03/29/government-as-a-platform-the-next-phase-of-digital-transformation/

82   NHS, *"Service Manual Design System"*, https://service-manual.nhs.uk/design-system

83   Tim Paul, *"Measuring the value of the GOV.UK Design System / Gov Design Meetup #14"*, February 2020 https://www.youtube.com/watch?v=eSkVtSEAe98

84   UK Government, *"Press release: Government's streamlined messaging service to save taxpayer £175m"*, September 2019 https://www.gov.uk/government/news/governments-streamlined-messaging-service-to-save-taxpayer-175m

85   Pete Herlihy, Tweet: Sharing latest Notify updates and stats https://twitter.com/yahoo_pete/status/1257701863832670209 and https://witter.com/yahoo_pete/status/1379516691923734528

86   Local Digital, *"Local Government Digital Declaration"* (267 organisations had signed this declaration as of October 2021) https://www.localdigital.gov.uk/declaration/

87   The Local Digital Fund was introduced in July 2018 by the then UK Local

Government Minister, Rishi Sunak, of the Department for Levelling Up, Housing and Communities (DLUHC).

88 Local Digital, *"Details of all funded projects (Local Digital Fund)"* https://www.localdigital.gov.uk/funded-projects/

89 BBC, *"Uber drivers are workers not self-employed, Supreme Court rules"*, February 2021 https://www.bbc.co.uk/news/business-56123668

90 Geoffrey G. Parker, Marshall W. Van Alstyne, Sangeet Paul Choudary, *"Platform Revolution: How Networked Markets Are Transforming the Economy and How to Make Them Work for You"*, W. W. Norton & Company, March 2016

91 Meal Makers (a subsidiary of the award winning Scottish charity Food Train) https://www.mealmakers.org.uk/

92 Definition adapted from: Richard W. DeVaul, *"Innovation isn't what you think it is"*, January 2019 https://devaul.medium.com/https-medium-com-devaul-innovation-isnt-what-you-think-it-is-52f03a9d2d7d

93 BBC, *"How Tower Hamlets council is tackling loneliness"*, November 2017 https://www.bbc.co.uk/news/uk-england-london-41685122

Chapter 6

94 Quote from: Doschka, Roland, *"Pablo Picasso: Metamorphoses of the Human Form: Graphic Works, 1895-1972"*, Prestel, 2000

95 UK Authority, *"Outdated IT contributed to underpayments of state pension"*, September 2021 https://www.ukauthority.com/articles/outdated-it-contributed-to-underpayments-of-state-pension/

96 GDS, *"You can't be half agile"*, July 2015 https://gds.blog.gov.uk/2015/07/10/you-cant-be-half-agile/

97 The Register, *"What's the price of failure? For Capita, it's a £140m extension to its MoD recruiting contract"*, December 2020 https://www.theregister.com/2020/12/14/capita_recruiting_partnership_project_140m_extension/

98 National Audit Office, *"Investigation into the British Army's Recruiting Partnering Project"*, December 2018 https://www.nao.org.uk/wp-content/uploads/2018/12/Investigation-into-the-British-Army-Recruiting-Partnering-Project.pdf

99 Estimated costs for NHS Jobs development provided in October 2021 by NHSBSA https://www.nhsbsa.nhs.uk

100 Wired Magazine, *"Elon Musk's Mission to Mars"*, October 2012 https://www.wired.com/2012/10/ff-elon-musk-qa/

101 Adapted from: Jon Kolko, *"Design is a mess"* https://www.modernisstudio.com/corporate-education/design-is-a-mess/

102 David Ayre, "*8 lenses of service transformation*", October 2021 https://www.tpximpact.com/insights/8-lenses-for-service-transformation

103 Hans Rosling, "*Factfullness: Ten Reasons We're Wrong About The World - And Why Things Are Better Than You Think*", Sceptre, June 2019

104 Kat Holmes, "*Mismatch: How Inclusion Shapes Design*", MIT Press, September 2020

Chapter 7

105 Quote attributed to Grace Hopper, American computer scientist and United States Navy rear admiral (1906-1992)

106 BBC, "*Syntax era: Sir Clive Sinclair's ZX Spectrum revolution*", December 2014 https://www.bbc.co.uk/news/technology-30333671

107 TPXimpact, "*Transforming Government Report*", April 2021 https://pages.tpximpact.com/en-gb/transforming-government-report-download

108 Hannah Fry, "*Hello World: How to be Human in the Age of the Machine*", Transworld Publishers Ltd,September 2019

109 Sarah Finch, "*3 minutes on RPA*", September 2021 https://www.tpximpact.com/insights/3-minutes-on-rpa

110 TPXimpact, "*Pharmacists back on the wards as NHS Wales automates*", September 2021 www.tpximpact.com/insights/pharmacists-back-on-the-wards-as-nhs-wales-automates

111 The Guardian, "*AI system outperforms experts in spotting breast cancer*", January 2020 https://www.theguardian.com/society/2020/jan/01/ai-system-outperforms-experts-in-spotting-breast-cancer

112 David Miller, Tweet, August 2018 https://twitter.com/thatdavidmiller/status/1026728268756606976

113 Ministry Of Justice, "*Technology at least as good as you have at home*", August 2016 https://mojdigital.blog.gov.uk/2016/08/02/technology-at-least-as-good-as-you-have-at-home/

114 TPXimpact, "*How technology can improve mental health patient care*", November 2021 https://www.tpximpact.com/insights/how-technology-can-improve-mental-health-patient-care

115 Sarah Finch, "*3 minutes on . . . Serverless*", December 2020 https://www.tpximpact.com/insights/3-minutes-on-serverless

116 Centre for Public Impact, "*Universal Credit System in the UK from 2010 to 2014*", September 2018 https://www.centreforpublicimpact.org/case-study/universal-credit-system-uk

117 UK Parliament, *"Universal credit: an end to the uplift"*, September 2021 https://lordslibrary.parliament.uk/universal-credit-an-end-to-the-uplift/

118 DWP Digital, *"DWP's agile response to COVID-19: scaling Universal Credit to meet demand"*, December 2020 https://dwpdigital.blog.gov.uk/2020/12/14/dwps-agile-response-to-covid-19-scaling-universal-credit-to-meet-demand/

119 Kayley Hignell, Tweet, October 2021 https://twitter.com/KayleyHignell/status/1453361192731385864

120 Sky News, *"Coronavirus: Intensive care patients given iPads to speak to relatives"*, April 2020 https://news.sky.com/story/coronavirus-intensive-care-patients-given-ipads-to-speak-to-relatives-11978509

121 TPXimpact, *"Young people's mental health"* https://www.tpximpact.com/our-work/nhsx-children-mental-health

Chapter 8

122 Alan Cooper, *"The Inmates are Running the Asylum: Why High-Tech Products Drive Us Crazy and How to Restore the Sanity"*, February 2004, Sams Publishing (first published March 1999)

123 TPXimpact, *"Transforming Government Report"*, April 2021 https://tpximact.com/6-key-digital-transformation-recommendations-for-a-modern-government Reference from http://news.bbc.co.uk/1/hi/8707355.stm

124 Michaell Brunton-Spall, Twitter thread, June 2021 https://twitter.com/bruntonspall/status/1405985374170669061

125 TPXimpact, *"Developing a shared vision for health & social care"* https://www.tpximpact.com/our-work/north-east-lincolnshire-adult-services

126 Christian Madsbjerg, *"Sensemaking: The Power of The Humanities in the Age of the Algorithm"*, Hachette Book Group, March 2017

127 Beacon https://beacon.support/

128 GDS, *"Government Digital Service: Our strategy for 2021-2024"*, May 2021 https://gds.blog.gov.uk/2021/05/20/government-digital-service-our-strategy-for-2021-2024/

129 Home Office, *"Our Home Office 2024 DDaT Strategy is published"*, May 2021 https://hodigital.blog.gov.uk/2021/07/12/our-home-office-2024-ddat-strategy-is-published/

130 Sarah Finch, *"Is the public sector doing enough with its data?"*, February 2021 https://www.tpximpact.com/insights/is-the-public-sector-doing-enough-with-its-data

131 Rikesh Shah, *"How TFL's Open Data is Driving Innovation in the UK"*, January 2017 https://www.youtube.com/watch?v=sZVnsvrIo4U

132 Transport for London, *"Transport for London Unified API"*, https://tfl.gov.uk/info-for/open-data-users/unified-api

133 Richard Pope, *"Real-time government"*, October 2018 https://medium.com/digitalhks/real-time-government-fd774b48e8a4

134 Forbes, *"What is Web 3.0"*, January 2020 https://www.forbes.com/sites/forbestechcouncil/2020/01/06/what-is-web-3-0/

135 E-Estonia, *"Estonia's KSI Blockchain"* https://e-estonia.com/solutions/cyber-security/ksi-blockchain/

136 Wired, *"Everything you need to know about the new NHS contact tracing app"*, October 2020 https://www.wired.co.uk/article/nhs-covid-19-tracking-app-contact-tracing

137 NHS Digital, "*General Practice Data for Planning and Research (GPDPR)"* https://digital.nhs.uk/data-and-information/data-collections-and-data-sets/data-collections/general-practice-data-for-planning-and-research

138 Citizens Advice, *"How we're working to transform the way we work with data - Making sure we get the basics right"*, January 2020 https://wearecitizensadvice.org.uk/how-were-working-to-transform-the-way-we-work-with-data-52a2de4def99

Chapter 9

139 The Guardian, *"Margaret Hamilton: 'They worried that the men might rebel. They didn't'"*, July 2019 https://www.theguardian.com/technology/2019/jul/13/margaret-hamilton-computer-scientist-interview-software-apollo-missions-1969-moon-landing-nasa-women

140 LocalGov Drupal https://localgovdrupal.org/

141 Fast Company, *"This House Costs Just $20,000—But It's Nicer Than Yours"*, March 2016 https://www.fastcompany.com/3056129/this-house-costs-just-20000-but-its-nicer-than-yours

142 GDS, *"What we've learnt about scaling agile"*, October 2012 https://gds.blog.gov.uk/2012/10/26/what-weve-learnt-about-scaling-agile/

143 Adapted from: Matthew Skelton, Manuel Pais, "*Team Topologies: Organizing Business and Technology Teams for Fast Flow"*, It Revolution Press, September 2019

144 Matt Edgar, *"The quick and the dead, or 6 things that change when your service goes live"*, September 2015 https://blog.mattedgar.com/2016/09/15/the-quick-and-the-dead-or-6-things-that-change-when-your-service-goes-live/

145 TPXimpact, *"Delivering the UK's COVID-19 home testing service"*, November 2021 http://www.tpximpact.com/our-work/delivering-the-uks-covid-19-home-testing-service

146 Terence Eden, *"Three Things I Wish I'd Known About NHS Technology"*, August 2012 https://shkspr.mobi/blog/2021/08/things-i-wish-id-known-about-nhs-technology/

147 GDS, *"We're changing the way we do service assessments to support coronavirus related services"*, April 2020 https://services.blog.gov.uk/2020/04/30/were-changing-the-way-we-do-service-assessments-to-support-coronavirus-related-services/

148 UK Government, *"Government Design Principles"* https://www.gov.uk/guidance/government-design-principles

149 NHS Integrated Care https://www.england.nhs.uk/integratedcare/

Chapter 10

150 Warren Buffet, 2008 letter to the Berkshire Hathaway Inc. shareholders https://www.berkshirehathaway.com/letters/2008ltr.pdf

151 Cabinet Office, *"Transforming Public Procurement Green Paper"*, December 2020 https://www.gov.uk/government/consultations/green-paper-transforming-public-procurement

152 The Lancet, *"Changes in cancer detection and false-positive recall in mammography using artificial intelligence: a retrospective, multireader study"*, February 2020 https://www.thelancet.com/journals/landig/article/PIIS2589-7500(20)30003-0/fulltext

153 UK Government, *"Digital, Data and Technology Profession"* https://www.gov.uk/government/organisations/digital-data-and-technology-profession

154 UK Government Commercial Function, *"The Social Value Model"*, December 2020 https://assets.publishing.service.gov.uk/government/uploads/system/uploads/attachment_data/file/940826/Social-Value-Model-Edn-1.1-3-Dec-20.pdf

155 Cabinet Office, *"Procurement Policy Note 06/21: Taking account of Carbon Reduction Plans in the procurement of major government contracts"*, June 2021 https://www.gov.uk/government/publications/procurement-policy-note-0621-taking-account-of-carbon-reduction-plans-in-the-procurement-of-major-government-contracts

156 TPXimpact, *"Planet"* https://investors.tpximpact.com/our-purpose/planet/

157 Google Cloud sustainability https://cloud.google.com/sustainability

Conclusion

158 Tony Benn (Editor: Ruth Winstone), *"The best of Benn"*, Hutchinson, November 2014

About Ben Holliday

Ben Holliday is Chief Designer at TPXimpact. With over 20 years' experience in design and digital transformation he works with organisations, change programmes and teams to deliver modern digital products and services.

Ben's experience in the public sector includes time as a civil servant, and design leadership roles at the Department for Work and Pensions as part of DWP Digital. Before this he worked with the Government Digital Service as part of the GDS Transformation programme of 25 exemplar projects.

In the private sector Ben has also worked extensively in digital, product and service delivery in the not-for-profit, charity, arts, education and financial sectors.

He lives in Kendal, Cumbria with his wife, their three daughters and son.

@BenHolliday
www.benholliday.com

About TPXimpact

TPXimpact partners with organisations across the public sector to deliver digital transformation that matters. With multidisciplinary teams working across technology, design, and digital experiences we are united by the belief that it's possible to deliver more – that by harnessing digital technologies, modern ways of working and a fresh mindset we can create better outcomes for people and the planet.

@tpximpact
www.tpximpact.com

Printed in Great Britain
by Amazon

78493080R00130